Can We Trust The New Testament?

JOHN A. T. ROBINSON

MOWBRAYS
LONDON & OXFORD

© A. R. Mowbray 1977

ISBN 0 264 66081 1

First published 1977
by A. R. Mowbray & Co Ltd,
The Alden Press, Osney Mead,
Oxford OX2 OEG

Text set in 11 pt Baskerville
and printed in Great Britain
by Richard Clay (The Chaucer Press), Ltd,
Bungay, Suffolk

Contents

INTRODUCTION

CAN we trust the New Testament? It's an odd question when you come to think of it. It's not a question that a Hindu would ask of the Bhagavad-Gita or a Muslim of the Koran or even a Jew of the Old Testament. Or if they did they would mean, Can you trust it as a guide to life, as the way to walk in? And this is a perfectly valid Christian question too. In fact a number of times in the so-called Pastoral Epistles (the brief letters written by Paul or in his name to Timothy and Titus) we have a phrase which means exactly this, 'Here are words you may trust' (New English Bible (NEB); in the Authorised or King James Version (AV): 'This is a faithful saying'). For the Christian message *is* offered as a faith and a way of life which you can trust. Indeed the primary purpose of the Gospels is succinctly put by St John when he says that he has written 'that you may *believe* that Jesus is the Christ, the Son of God, and that believing you may have *life* in his name' (John 20.31). But of this 'word of life' the same man says, 'We have heard it; we have seen it with our own eyes; we looked upon it, and felt it with our own hands' (1 John 1.1). And there lies the difference. For 'the way, the truth and the life' for the writers of the New Testament is not a timeless prescription for good living but a person born at a moment of history. And trusting the New Testament is trusting it for a portrait of that person.

7

A portrait, not a photograph. And a portrait not of a dead man, but of one who was for its writers now and for ever the human face of *God*. Yet if that portrait turned out to bear no relation to the sitter behind it, to the historical individual they claimed to have seen and heard and handled, then they would on their own confession be found liars. You cannot 'trust the New Testament' without trusting the claim at its very heart that it is not just an imaginary picture but a faithful portrait—full of faith, to be sure, but true also to fact.

Now you cannot test that claim without being prepared to go to history, and therefore to the methods of historical inquiry and verification. And these methods are neutral to the faith: they cannot be guaranteed to reinforce it. There is always the risk that the results of the investigation may turn out negative. And at best none of the answers in any historical inquiry will be more than extremely probable: even the existence of Napoleon or Julius Caesar is not a matter of absolute certainty. Many religious people therefore have feared and distrusted these methods. They have thought to settle questions of history—whether, for instance, Jesus said or did this or that—not by the historical evidence, but by assertions of faith. In this they have shown themselves to be obscurantists—and left the tools of historical investigation to the faithless. The Church owes a great debt to its scholars over the past two hundred years who have refused to do this. They have been prepared to accept the risks. In the process 'the critics', as they have come to be called, have often appeared to the faithful to be doubtful allies—if not downright traitors. Indeed there is a fatal ambiguity in the phrase 'biblical criticism', since it appears to mean being critical *of* the Bible, and therefore destructive. In fact it means using one's critical faculties *on* the Bible like any other book—and its results can be entirely positive, confirming rather than undermining.

But it is too early yet to worry about results. This book is an invitation to trust, to go hand in hand with the scholar to the New Testament, to see what he is up to and watch him as he goes about his work. And the first thing to recognise is that no scholar comes to his work without his presuppositions. He does not start with a blank mind but with one formed by all the influences, beliefs and convictions that have made him what he is. In this he is just like the rest of us. Hence it is not surprising that in this as in every other field of knowledge experts differ, and differ widely. This is bewildering to the layman, whose reaction is not to know whom to trust and therefore to trust no one. In fact such is the confusion of voices in this field that many have lost the confidence that there is any agreed truth to arrive at. So they either give up believing anything or become reinforced in their judgement that they know what they believe and the less they let 'the critics' near it the better. Both of these reactions I hope to show are fundamentally faithless and unjustified.

In a book like this I could have followed one of two methods. I could have surveyed the conflicting opinions, said what everyone *else* believes and kept my own judgement out of it (though it would not really have been out of it). Or I could, as I have done, present one man's view, while trying at the same time to be fair to those from whom I would differ and warning the reader where there would be general agreement and where there would not. Since therefore my own presuppositions will not be suppressed, I had better state where I stand.

This is somewhat against the stream of what I

suppose would be called current critical orthodoxy in the field of New Testament scholarship. I would be more conservative—on some issues much more conservative—than most of my colleagues who are prepared to use the same methods. Since this may surprise many of my readers, who may regard me by reputation as a dangerous radical, let me try to describe, as I see it, the lie of the field.

Confining myself for the moment to the English scene—the Continental and the American reflect greater extremes—I observe two poles of thought between which there is constant interaction. One of these tends to be fairly radical—and sceptical—about what may be accepted as historically trust-worthy in the New Testament, though with it can go quite a strong traditionalism in doctrinal belief and churchmanship. The most extreme example I have met of this—he was an American—was a professor who accepted nothing in the birth narratives of the Gospels as remotely historical but combined this with the 'highest' possible belief in the virgin birth, the immaculate conception and anything else you liked to mention. It seemed to me schizo-phrenic, but not to him. In a less extreme manner it is obviously possible to have honest doubts about much in the historical tradition and yet to retain a lively and orthodox Christian faith. I remember once a theological college principal saying what a comfort the radical German New Testament scholar Bultmann was to him. For whenever he was being driven back and back and thought he had nothing left on which to base his faith, he looked behind him and there was Bultmann, and *he* hadn't gone over the precipice yet! A man in this position may be able to 'get by 'on a good deal less about the Jesus of history than most people would think they needed in order to remain Christian. And in the pastoral ministry this can lead to a fairly sophisticated scepticism at the scholarly level combined with quite traditional preaching and liturgical practice at the popular level. For there are things that may be true for the cognoscenti—but the faithful must not be needlessly disturbed. This has been a feature especially of much liberal catholicism, both Roman Catholic and Anglican.

Now this not a position in which I find myself, and I do not think I could hold it for long if I did. On purely critical grounds I am far more convinced of the trustworthiness of the historical tradition. This is simply the way the evidence seems to me to point. But then I want to go on to ask some fairly radical questions about how we can make our own and use that tradition and its language today. For instance, on the virgin birth or the resurrection, though I would want above all to discriminate about how much fact is involved and how much interpretation, I would come to relatively conservative conclusions, particularly on the resurrection. (I will say where I stand later.) But that does not mean that we may not need to rethink pretty drastically how we can make the New Testament tradition meaningful today. For instance, what does it really mean to say that Jesus is 'the son of God' or 'pre-existent' in a world like ours where those sort of categories are alien, *as they weren't in the first century*, to the way in which ordinary people think or talk? Just to go on repeating them as they stand may convey nothing—or something subtly different.

The corollary of this position is that I do *not* want to protect ordinary people from what the scholars are saying, but precisely to expose them. I want to put them in the picture, so that when they come, as they must, to work out for themselves what they can believe today they may do it as far as possible with the benefit of the best knowledge available. For the best knowledge I do not believe to be shattering to faith—even if it is at first disturbing to ignorance. For the results of what has gone through the finest critical sieve that has ever been applied to any literature I find encouraging. Of course there is much that does not survive—and *everything* must be allowed to be put in question if it is to be truly tested. But I want to share these results, and to try to bridge the dangerous gap that has grown up between the professor and the pulpit and the pew. The faults have by no means all been with one party, but ignorance breeds mistrust. It is that mistrust at all levels that I should like to hope this book may do a little to dissipate.

television two recent books on the New Testament. Both were by professors. One was a popular book of profound simplicity and maturity, distilling the reading and teaching of a lifetime, written by one of the greatest English-speaking New Testament scholars of this generation. It paraded no learning, cited no authorities, trailed no footnotes. The other was by a professor in a completely different field. He had obviously done his homework and he buttressed his arguments with extensive references and quotations. The trouble was that his chief source had evidently been an encyclopaedia published some seventy years earlier, which even in its day could hardly be said to represent a particularly balanced judgement and which no student would now dream of consulting as an authority. I confess I did not read his book through, which was quite substantial, but I thought I would test it by checking his views on a half-dozen leading English New Testament scholars in the subject. Not one was even mentioned in the index or in his bibliography of nearly three hundred titles.

I mention this not to criticise *him* (to be fair, he has since followed it up with a much better researched though equally unbalanced volume). I should doubtless have made much the same gaffs had I been so bold, or so foolish, to write in his field. Nor did it altogether surprise me that my TV interviewer was far more impressed by the parade of learning in the second book, and with its, to him, novel and shattering thesis that Jesus never existed or was to all intents and purposes the creation of the early Christians. What did shake me, however, was that it carried a promotional puff from a professor of modern history, with a world-wide reputation, commending its 'exact historical method and wide and up-to-date knowledge'. And this highly

14

TREVOR-ROPER

professional historian then went on to review the
other book in a national weekly, where he accused
its author of 'textual fundamentalism modified by
convenience'. He spoke of the 'gulfs of oblivious
mythopaeic time' which separate the New Testament writings from the events they claim to record
and made the astonishing statement that 'no Gospel
text can be traced even indirectly back beyond the
fourth century AD'. 'The plain fact is,' he said, 'that
we know nothing about the historical Christ. If we
believe that he existed, it is not because the Gospels
tell us so. The Gospels, after all, tell us a lot of palp-
able rubbish.'

This might be ignored as the lapse of an individual who should have known better, were it not
part of a widespread tendency to accept in the area
of Christian origins judgements and constructions
that anywhere else would be laughed out of court.
There has been a whole series of titles such as *The
Nazarene Gospel Restored*, *The Passover Plot*, *The
Sacred Mushroom*, presented to the public by reput-
able publishers as serious historical contributions.
It is hardly surprising that confidence has been
eroded in our capacity now to say anything objective
at all. When a sympathetic scientist writing on
popular Christianity can say that preference for
another view of Jesus over that of *The Sacred
Mushroom* is 'only speculation on my part', he is
saying that the sort of controls that he would apply
anywhere in his field just do not exist here. This
represents the abdication of the scientific method,
not its conclusion.

This attitude is but the other side of the penny
of the view that if you can't believe everything you
can't believe anything—that if Alfred and the cakes
isn't factual, then every historical statement is likely
to be as true or false as any other. This is not a re-

sponse we should adopt anywhere else. It is in fact part of the backlash to the second attitude we must go on to consider, which has again been stronger and more persistent here than in any other field.

THE FUNDAMENTALISM OF THE FEARFUL

Fundamentalism, as an 'ism', is an astonishingly modern phenomenon—dating from since the first world war (the word occurs only in the Supplement of the Oxford English Dictionary, being first recorded in 1923!). Though the conservative attitude it buttresses is of course as old as the hills, it came in as an 'ism' as a reaction of fear to nineteenth- and early twentieth-century biblical criticism—and there was plenty in the wilder extremes to which that swung to induce if not to justify the fear. But the answer to bad criticism was, as the great English biblical scholars like Lightfoot, Westcott and Hort saw, better criticism, not none. The defensive response was however to close the hatches, and both the Roman Catholic and sections of the Protestant Churches tended to seek refuge in a verbal inspirationism which depended on the all or nothing mentality we have mentioned. If every syllable in the Bible represented the direct dictation of the Holy Ghost, there could be no place in it for error of any kind. Once admit the slightest possibility that anything might not be literally true or the actual words of our Lord, and where would you stop? Indeed, unless you had some other criteria, where could you stop? You might end up with nothing left to believe. This fear has always been one of the strengths—and of course weaknesses—of the fundamentalist position. I have often said that the fundamentalist and the radical share the same concern—to go to the foundations or roots. But it is not accidental that the one uses an inorganic and the other an organic

16

metaphor. Digging around foundations can have a very different effect from digging around roots: dislodge one stone and the entire building may collapse.

I recall a student contemporary of mine telling me the point at which he was forced to give up such a verbal inspirationist view of the Bible. If every word, every syllable, every letter was inspired, then in the Hebrew of the Old Testament you must obviously believe that the vowel-pointings were authenticated in the same way. Otherwise the consonants by themselves could obviously, as in English, be made to form very different words, yielding sometimes an entirely different sense. For example, in Isa. 49.17 the AV reads 'thy children', the RSV (Revised Standard Version) 'your builders': it simply depends on which vowel you supply. But the vowel-pointings were not written in any ancient Hebrew manuscripts; they were supplied in the reading of it and passed on by oral tradition. They were finally codified in an 'official' text by Jewish scribes of the ninth and tenth centuries AD, and it is this text that is translated in the AV. A good and careful job they did, though variations in any modern version of the Old Testament will frequently depend on judgements about how a word should be 'pointed', i.e., what vowels should be inserted between the consonants. (This does not apply to the New Testament as the vowels in Greek, as in English, were always written.) The dilemma in which my friend found himself was that if the text of the Old Testament was inspired by God 'just as it left him', then he must have inspired these mediaeval Jewish rabbis with the same inerrant judgement—or the entire exercise would have been frustrated: one would never know what he 'really' said. But this meant attributing to them an infallibility which he would not have dreamt of attributing to the Fathers of the Christian Church. The contradiction was too great, and he was compelled to abandon the assumption on which it rested. Yet so far from everything collapsing, he came through like so many like him to a much more widely and deeply based Christian conviction, whose strength is far less brittle and includes the freedom to sift and to test *everything*.

Literalist fundamentalism of this narrow sort has in my experience, at any rate in the student world where it was once very strong, almost, though not entirely, disappeared. Like the Roman Catholics, whose Pontifical Biblical Commission has effectively gone into reverse (without, of course, actually saying so), the Conservative Evangelicals have changed much more than most of them would admit. There are still indeed blinkers and blockages and some fairly powerful hang-ups. It is still difficult, for instance, for them even to be open to the possibility that Jesus might have been mistaken on anything. A stock example of this is the authorship of Psalm 110. In a typically rabbinic argument in Mark 12.35–7 Jesus cites the first verse of this psalm, 'The Lord said to my Lord'. The point he makes depends on 'David himself' having said it—for how, he argues, can the Messiah be David's 'son' if *he himself* calls him 'Lord'? Yet it is probable (or at least possible) that this psalm comes not from David's time but from hundreds of years later. But the ascription to David simply shows Jesus to be a true Jew of the first century. If he had any *other* view of the authorship of the psalms, or the motion of the planets, or the cause of epilepsy, he would not have been. It is entirely compatible with Christian belief that he could (by our standards) have been mistaken on this and other factual matters and still be the Word of God to that generation—and to ours.

Or take another point where the fundamentalist is on the horns of a dilemma—Jesus's reported predictions about the end of the world coming in his generation. Now *if* he said this, and his words are to be interpreted literally, then clearly he was wrong —and the possibility of this would be accepted by the main stream of both Catholic and Protestant scholars today. Once more it would mean that he thought and spoke in the categories of that form of contemporary Jewish thinking, which we call apocalyptic, that did believe that God would intervene and bring things to a head very shortly. On the other hand, it is possible—I would think probable —that his words have been adapted and interpreted to fit such ways of thinking in the early Church. In this case our Bibles do not contain what Jesus said or meant.

The point is that neither possibility can be ruled out in advance. If one then asks, Well, how do we know what Jesus said and what is to be put down to the early Church?, the only way to assess the probabilities (we shall never get certainty) is to go to the evidence, as the archaeologist would go to the strata in his dig or the picture-restorer to the layers of superimposed paint, and patiently reconstruct what is likely to be most original. We shall later be having a closer look at this process and the methods available. But for now it is enough to recognise that Jesus may indeed have been reinterpreted or misinterpreted by his friends. So what? Unless we are *free* to admit this is a possibility and then to sift and sort out where and how it has happened, we shall not be able to meet those who say that we can know nothing—or even that there is nothing underneath at all.

So far we have been looking at two positions that are poles apart yet which meet as extremes often do. Indeed one is the obverse of the other, and they have only each other to blame—which for the most part is about all they ever do. But there are two further attitudes, both powerful within the Church, which coexist in a relationship of tolerant yet guarded suspicion.

THE SCEPTICISM OF THE WISE

It is difficult to write about this without seeming to sound depreciatory. But scepticism like criticism is an ambiguous word. The first definition of 'sceptical' in the dictionary is 'inclined to suspense of judgement, given to questioning truth of facts and soundness of inferences'. The word comes from the Greek for to 'examine', and, as Plato said long ago, the unexamined life is not worth living. To suspend judgement, to question, is the proper attitude of the philosopher and the scholar; and the Church should be grateful for it in her scholars. To take history seriously, for instance, is not to believe everything in the tradition. You may indeed take history more seriously by saying that Alfred and the cakes is *not* history but legend. Similarly in the Gospels the scholar does not take everything 'as gospel'. He discriminates. He recognises that there are different sorts of statement, different levels of truth, in this as in all other literature. There are purely factual statements and there are statements designed to give the interpretation of the facts. And this interpretation may be given through a variety of means—for instance, by recognised poetic imagery or symbolism (such as sitting on the right hand of God, or clouds of glory, or angels) or by imaginatively told stories (like that of the star stopping over where the young child was: you have merely to look up at a star to

20

realise that it can't literally stop *over* anything). Their purpose is to open up new dimensions within the history. But to talk of 'myth' or 'legend', as scholars do in any field, is to appear to ordinary people to be saying that it is *not* true. And the difficulty deepens when you try to discriminate and disentangle just what is true at what level, what is bare fact and what is myth or word-picture to deepen and draw out its meaning—as for instance, in the accounts of the birth or the resurrection or the ascension of Jesus. Peeling back the layers of interpretation *looks* like a process of reduction, and the feeling gets around that 'they' have left us very little. The 'sceptics' who began as neutral are seen as threats to the faith: 'they have taken away my Lord, and I know not where they have laid him'.

As we go on we shall have to look at these things in greater detail and try to interpret one side to the other. But at this point I would want to say that in the gap between the scholar and the layman the faults are not all on the side of the latter. There is, I believe, an undue scepticism of the wise, which, perhaps by overcompensation, seems especially characteristic of biblical scholars. They are so conscious of the fact that they are dealing not with 'straight' history but with what, before it became a dirty word, could be called 'propaganda' (as in 'the Society for the Propagation of the Gospel'), that the discount they introduce is the greater. Thus we are reminded constantly, and absolutely rightly, that the Gospels are not biographies. That is to say, they are not primarily written from the point of view of what any biographer would properly be interested in. (It has been observed, for instance, that they never think to tell us whether Jesus was married— or, if he wasn't, to say so.) Rather, they are 'gospels', good news about God, and everything in them is given this slant. They tell us primarily about what *the Church* was interested in preaching and teaching. Similarly the Book of Acts is not straight history: it is 'the gospel of the Holy Spirit'. The tendency therefore both outside and inside the Church has been to regard these as 'loaded' sources, and New Testament scholars have often seemed to lean over backwards not to appear less sceptical than the rest. This at any rate is how it has looked to some entering the field from another discipline. For instance, C. S. Lewis, coming from English literature, once gave a talk to theological students on 'Modern Theology and Biblical Criticism' (now reprinted in his *Christian Reflections*) in which he enjoyed himself at the expense of biblical scholars who are so busy looking between the lines that they never see what is on them. 'Everywhere, except in theology,' he said, 'there has been a vigorous growth of scepticism about scepticism itself.' Yet his own approach, which was confessedly that of the layman in the field, had much of the fourth and last attitude about it which we shall go on to describe, and indeed is a good example of how the two can provoke and rile each other. More impressive is the judgement of A. N. Sherwin-White, the Oxford classical historian, who in his *Roman Society and Roman Law in the New Testament* chides New Testament scholars for failing to recognise what by any comparable standards excellent sources they have!

In this matter so much can turn on where a scholar puts the burden of proof. If you ask, Is there any reason why Jesus should *not* have said or done this?, you may find very little reason why he should not, and your conclusion will be positive. If you ask, Is there any reason why Jesus *should* have said or done this?, you may find equally little reason why he should, and your conclusion will be negative.

Adopt one or the other approach all the way through, and the resulting picture will be dramatically different, although neither question is in itself more scholarly than the other. Thus, in the contemporary German scene, the great New Testament scholar Rudolf Bultmann tended to start with the question that leads to the negative conclusion, laying the burden of proof on those who would claim that such and such a saying, for example, 'You are Peter, and on this rock I will build my church' (Matt. 16.18), has its origin in Jesus rather than the Christian community. The equally great New Testament scholar Johachim Jeremias tends to start with the question that leads to the positive conclusion, noting the Palestinian background to the phrasing and asking why it should not be dominical. Neither for that reason is more scientific in his approach than the other.

Yet it is not simply a matter of 'you pays your money and you takes your choice'. I believe there are certain *false* assumptions and deductions written into the negative attitude which make it unwarrantably sceptical. Thus, you can say, quite rightly, that the New Testament writings, Gospels as well as Epistles, tell us a great deal about the early Christian communities for whose purposes and needs they were written. They allow us to see what were *their* interests and concerns—in preaching, teaching, liturgy, discipline and the rest—which made them select and slant what they recorded of Jesus so as to meet and serve these ends. But it is easy to slide from that recognition into the conclusion that the *more* they tell us about the early church the *less* they tell us about Jesus, and even to end up by saying that you cannot get behind the early Church at all. Yet this is logically fallacious.

Let me illustrate this by a modern example.

George Orwell wrote a collection of what he called *Critical Essays*, in which he started from the question, What does this literature tell us, not of the things it is written about, but of the socio-economic attitudes of those who wrote it? He brought this approach in a most illuminating and entertaining manner to a whole range of 'literature' from Dickens and Kipling to Boys' Weeklies and seaside postcards. The question he put is one that can be applied to anything, including the New Testament. But to put it does not rule out or even diminish the fact that the writings concerned may also tell us a great deal about the subject they are meant to be on. Indeed an analysis of the writers' largely unconscious class assumptions may enable us the better to *discount* the distorting influence of these on their subject-matter. Similarly, in the study of the Gospels, the more we know of the factors, conscious and unconscious, that gave the early Christians an interest in applying and adapting the life and teaching of Jesus to their own message and conflicts, the better position we are in to discount these influences, and, as it were, strip away that superimposed layer. We can see also what there is *no* reason to think they would have introduced, and this actually strengthens rather than diminishes our confidence in getting back to Jesus. The whole process may end in telling us more about him rather than less.

Or let me give another example of what seems to me unwarranted scepticism. One technique that has been used in recent New Testament criticism is applying to the teaching of Jesus the test of 'dissimilarity'. Is there anything, it asks, that *cannot* be put down to the Judaism out of which he came or to the Christian Church which took him over? If so, it may confidently be attributed to him. This, as I

24

have already suggested, is obviously a useful test. But if made the sole or even the dominant criterion, it does not take much to see that it reduces all that we can be sure he said to what *no one else* said before or since. If one applied that test to any other great man or creative teacher, not only would one be left with very little indeed but one would unquestionably distort him by isolating him from his times. For originality so often consists in drawing out what was there all the time and in inspiring what others immediately recognise and take up. A man has to come upon his hour in order to say anything to it.

We must return to many of these questions, and I shall be wishing to take issue also on a number of purely factual points with what I have called this scepticism of the wise—for instance, with what seems to me the excessively long 'tunnel period' they envisage during which the traditions about the life and teaching of Jesus were lost to sight before they finally emerged (by then uncheckable) in our Gospels. But here I would simply record it among the attitudes to be taken into account, especially since the assumptions I have mentioned have tended to dominate some of the most widely read paperback commentaries. But this attitude again has to be set and understood against its shadow-image, to which lastly we must turn.

THE CONSERVATISM OF THE COMMITTED

Despite all the storms and waves that have gone over it, there remains, especially in England, a deep mass of water that has steadfastly refused to be shifted by anything much that has happened on the surface. This body of opinion is not fundamentalist, but it is conservative; and it really hasn't *believed* what the critics have been saying. The winds of fashion come and go, but the committed have their anchors and are content to ride out the storm. Of course in the process they are changed more than they think and certain things are silently modified. But there is a supple strength in this attitude such as is traditionally supposed to serve and to save the Chinese: bend before the gale and when it has passed over you you can stand upright again.

It can be illustrated best in the area of the New Testament by the ordinary lay Christian's attitude to 'the Fourth Gospel'. The very title indeed is a bit of scholarly affectation. For no one talks in ordinary speech about the First or other Gospels. But critical susceptibilities have been respected to the extent of allowing the scholars this circumlocution, though it is certainly no more agreed among them (in fact even less) that St Matthew wrote St Matthew than that St John wrote St John. But apart from the question of authorship there is a stubborn conviction among the silent majority that has refused to let the critics 'take away' St John. All the time that the scholars have been telling them that St John's Gospel is, of course, factually quite unreliable and that its picture of Jesus is simply a mystical meditation of much religious but of no historical value, they have quietly bided their time. And they are beginning to look like being justified. This is not to commend their critical faculties, which have largely been dormant. But it is to draw attention to their horse-sense.

No one can both be a teacher in the university and a preacher in the Church without being aware of the strong conservative 'undertow' in the country at large. The 'reassuring' sermon is that which tells people that they can after all believe that Jesus said or did what he is supposed to have said or done, that the Christmas story is 'true', that the tomb was empty and that 'the critics' have been proved un-founded. For such people, whether clergy or laity, who from time to time break out in letters to *The Times* or *The Church Times*, scholarship is basic-ally a threat to be weathered. I believe that in many of their conclusions (if not in the way they reach them) they are right, and I discover that the sermons that I preach on these questions often take people agreeably by surprise. In fact the upshot of this book will probably seem to many of my critics un-expectedly, perhaps suspiciously, conservative. Par-ticularly on St John I find I have long had strange allies—I remember being sent an article by a Southern Baptist from the United States who was using me, I think in all innocence, as a stick with which to beat the liberals! On the dating of the New Testament (as will become evident) I derive a certain innocent merriment from outflanking my more conservative pupils when they serve up what the textbooks say. Yet for all this, I believe that the conservatism of the committed is a seriously re-actionary force in the field, and I would never dream of abetting the obscurantism of those letters. It too can generate its opposite and contribute to the kind of polarisation that seldom in my experience produces more light than heat.

For like the fundamentalism of the fearful, it takes cover behind a suspicion of scholarship—except, that is, where this is thought to come out the 'right' way, when its 'assured results' (usually stated with far too much confidence) are triumphantly cited to prove that after all 'the Bible is true'. Yet the only healthy attitude can be to trust to impartial scholarly investigation *whichever* way it comes out. For those who are genuinely committed to Christ as the truth must be prepared for the risk which God himself took when he committed himself to history,

that is, to the contingency of events and to the falli-
bility of records. They more than others must believe that 'great is truth and it shall prevail' and
never be tempted or driven back into equating orthodoxy with ignorance: that way lies betrayal and
defeat.

For positions that look safe in a storm may turn
out to be dubious refuges. A hundred years ago the
conservatism of the committed was quite sure where
the defence of the faith lay. It lay with Bishop
Samuel Wilberforce and his allies in insisting that
the opening chapters of Genesis were literally and
historically true: to allow that they could be true as
myths, while Darwin's views could also be true as
science, was to sell out. Yet had these good men won
the day against Thomas Huxley and his allies, it
would be impossible now to be a Christian *and* a
scientist. The cause of the faith would have suffered
irreparable damage—whereas in fact the stories of
the creation and the fall have now been liberated to
become far more meaningful than when they were
true simply of a single remote period of time. The
truth of the Gospel stories involves indeed a more
complex interrelationship of fact and interpretation—for Jesus, unlike Adam, *was* a historical individual. The task of disentangling the strands in
them demands therefore greater critical discrimination, not less. The *way* in which we can 'trust' the
New Testament is less simple than the way in
which we can trust the Old Testament, let alone the
Koran or the Bhagavad-Gita. For the 'mix' in the
Christ-event is richer. It calls for the full alliance of
conviction and criticism, not their mutual distanc-
ing in guarded distrust.

The conservatism of the committed is probably
more entrenched in the sort of people likely to read
this book—and, if I am honest, deep down in

myself—than any of the other attitudes. It therefore behoves us to be especially wary, and respectful, of it. The plea is often heard not to 'disturb' the faithful or make it 'all too complicated'. 'Why can't you leave us alone?'—or at any rate leave the Bible alone. In a simpler, pre-scientific age this might have been enough—as it doubtless is for millions of people still, in many parts of the globe. Yet we live, for good or for ill, especially those of us who read paperbacks and watch television, in a world where everything *else* is being questioned; and in an increasingly revolutionary society a pre-critical faith will come to be seen as a harmless if beautiful relic. It is sobering to reflect that it is mainly in those areas of Christendom where biblical criticism has made least impact, in eastern Orthodoxy and peasant Catholicism, that Marxism has made most. This is *not* a reason for doing biblical criticism: indeed the most militantly fundamentalist are often the most blindly anti-communist! But it could help to shake us out of our dogmatic slumbers—if the sight does not do so of so many thousands of young people merely passing us by. Moreover the resurgence of fundamentalist attitudes in our day, even in educated countries and in charismatic circles that supposedly prize the spirit above the letter, speaks judgement on the churches for failing to present an intelligent authority of the Bible as a viable alternative to non-biblical spiritualities. But the best and ultimately the only valid reason for taking the quest seriously is the love and trust of truth for its own sake, which means, for the Christian, for Christ's sake. And that, with *whichever* predisposing attitude we may begin, is finally the sole test and judge of us all.

2

FACTS AND FALLACIES

ONE of the most powerful factors in distrust is ignorance, and I find in talking to laymen that there are all kinds of misconceptions about the New Testament, and what scholars do, that lay them open to believing anything—or nothing. So it may be useful to start with an elementary collection of facts and fallacies to clear the ground on which to build.

THE ORIGINAL LANGUAGE
The New Testament consists of twenty-seven separate 'books'—and is therefore better thought of as a library-shelf than a book. All of them were originally written in Greek. I mention this because some people think that the Epistle to the Hebrews must be written in Hebrew, and even the Epistle to the Romans in Latin. But 'Hebrews' only means Jewish Christians, and throughout the eastern half of the Roman empire and indeed in Rome itself the international language, the *lingua franca* in which most exchange was conducted, was Greek. This was a result of the conquests of Alexander the Great some three centuries earlier, and in the heart of Palestine, which was once part of his empire, it is becoming clear that Greek was commonly used as a second language even by quite ordinary people. There is no mention of an interpreter in the Gospels, and Pilate, for instance, would almost certainly have

conducted his conversations with the Jews and with Jesus in Greek. This is relevant when we come to ask whether so-called 'Galilean peasants', like Peter and John and James the Lord's brother, could themselves have written the books that stand against their names. The evidence is accumulating to suggest that they could. Whether they did, of course, is another matter and raises much wider issues. But it *is* significant that all the early Christian writings, including those that evidently have a Palestinian background, are in Greek. And this is the more significant when practically all the writings from the Dead Sea caves produced by the Qumran community at the same time or a little earlier are in Hebrew. Neither language was that of the people, which was Aramaic, a member of the same family of languages as Hebrew. It was not, as is commonly supposed, a late dialect form of Hebrew. If you look at the footnote to Gen. 31.47 in the NEB you will see that even then Jacob is represented as speaking Hebrew, Laban Aramaic. But in the times between the Testaments (as part of the book of Daniel shows, which was written then) and in the New Testament period Aramaic was the speech of Palestine. Hebrew would still have been used for 'high' purposes, for the liturgy and Scripture reading, but there were paraphrases of the Old Testament in the vernacular for synagogue use.

Jesus certainly would have given his teaching in Aramaic, and so, except where the occasional word has been transliterated into Greek like *abba* (the child's word he used for addressing God as 'Dad'), we do not have any of his actual speech—and of course he didn't *write* anything himself. This then is the first missing link in the chain of transmission. How do we know that the Greek translations have not got him wrong? The answer is, of course, that we cannot be certain. Indeed there are places where differences in Gospel sayings look like translation variants. For instance, 'Be perfect, as your heavenly Father is perfect' (Matt. 5.48) and 'Be merciful, even as your Father is merciful' (Luke 6.36) have plausibly been argued to be alternative translations of a single Aramaic word meaning 'whole' or 'generous'. Others too have suggested that behind the baffling phrase, for which no satisfactory parallel has yet been found, 'Behold, the Lamb of God, who takes away the sin of the world!' (John 1.29), may lie a mistranslation (or a double meaning) of the Aramaic for 'the servant of God'. Yet the mere fact that these reconstructions can be guessed at shows how near beneath the surface of the Greek the Aramaic still lies—especially in those parts of the teaching of Jesus (like much of the Sermon on the Mount) which are in poetic form, with its Semitic parallelism, rhythm and even rhyme. Though we cannot recover the *ipsissima verba*, the actual words of Jesus, some (like the German scholar Jeremias I mentioned earlier) are convinced that at many points we can hear the *ipsissima vox*, the distinctive voice of the Master.

The first gap in the chain is therefore not nearly as great as might at first appear. It is doubtful if much of the record is seriously affected or distorted merely by the language barrier—especially since so many were bilingual. This does not of course mean that in Greek dress the teaching of Jesus has not become subtly adapted to the conditions of a different milieu. His words or actions, for instance, may have become modified to fulfil or bear out the Greek version of the Old Testament (the Septuagint or LXX —so named because of the legend that it was translated, independently, by seventy scholars). Certain prophecies only 'work' if they are read in the Septuagint version—e.g., most famously, Isa. 7.14, quoted in Matt. 1.23, where the Hebrew means merely that 'a young woman' will conceive, not 'a virgin'. Sometimes, too, we can detect minor changes in expression, especially in the Gospel of Luke, which arise from its being addressed to the gentile culture of the Graeco–Roman world. Thus in Luke 5.19, in contrast with Mark 2.4, the roof has tiles, which makes the process of penetrating it a good deal more formidable! But all this is part of the much larger and more important question, to which we must return, of how Jesus's teaching was reapplied in very different circumstances to the mission and message of the early Church.

MANUSCRIPTS AND MISTAKES

Meanwhile, there is the second and far longer gap, not between what Jesus said and what he is recorded as saying, but between that record and the state in which it has reached us. The Gospels, like all ancient books, were of course written by hand, originally on scrolls but soon afterwards in codex or book form, and then laboriously copied by a succession of scribes, in the earliest times on papyrus, the predecessor of our paper (most of which inevitably has perished), and then on vellum or parchment, made from animals' skins. How do we know that in the process the record has not changed beyond recognition, as in a game of consequences, by the compounding of mistakes?

First one must say that the analogy is misleading. Transmission, even by word of mouth, was a much more exact and controlled process than it is for us, with teachers trained and instructed by their masters to memorise their words and pass them on with an astonishing degree of accuracy. Then the scribe, who was a professional, was much more like the modern copy-typist or proof-reader than the amateur playing a game. We can recognise—and so discount—the kind of errors that frequently recur. One, to which a modern secretary is equally liable, is that the eye drops from a word or clause which ends in one way to another in a following line which ends in the same way—so that in this last sentence, for instance, everything between the two words 'way' gets left out. In fact that happened in the final typing of a draft of the NEB, and a whole verse got accidentally omitted! However, it was picked up in the process, and this illustrates the important fact that the transmission of copy is not the work of one man. There were schools of scribes, as later there were in the monasteries, and the greatest care was taken in checking, often by counting the lines and letters. Our biggest safeguard however is the many-stranded cord of transmission. In the case of some ancient authors everything literally hangs on the thread of a single manuscript. In the case of the New Testament there are hundreds and indeed thousands of threads—and of course correspondingly numerous variations. Naturally some threads are much older and more valuable than others—and most of the variations frankly insignificant. A copy cannot have more authority than that from which it was taken—though it may often be useful if it was produced by comparing and collating manuscripts of different family origin. The science or art of textual criticism is concerned with tracing the family trees, explaining how the variants are likely to have arisen and trying to work back as near to source as possible (the original autographs having of course perished).

So much work has been done on this over so long a time that a considerable body of established results has been built up—though this does not mean that here, as elsewhere, the judgements of experts do not differ. Printed editions of the Greek text are readily available with the main variants at the foot of the page for easy comparison. I mention this because I find that the popular image of the New Testament scholar, or even of the Bible translator, is of a man poring over ancient manuscripts (and of having his work constantly upset by the discovery of new ones). But there is no need of this except for the palaeographic expert, with his (now) expensive machinery. (It is said that a modern university became convinced that theology was after all a science when its first professor in the subject—who happened to be a textual critic—began by ordering a whole load of photographic equipment, and then put in for a building in which to house it!) But the rest of us can rely on this microscopic work to be done for us. And though important new manuscripts do turn up from time to time, constantly refining the process and closing the gap, it is highly unlikely that in the New Testament any will come up with even one entirely new reading which must obviously be accepted as original.

Perhaps it is worth just interjecting a word here on the Dead Sea scrolls, discovered in 1947, which have been the most exciting and most publicised find in recent years. None of the caves, of course, contained a single text of the New Testament, for the monastery of Qumran was a Jewish not a Christian community. (Press reports a few years back of minute Greek fragments of New Testament books have proved to be unsubstantiated, and in any case these would have been later deposits.) There were many scrolls and fragments of major importance for establishing the text of the *Old* Testament, narrowing the gap between the original writing and our earliest manuscripts by several centuries. But their effect on the whole has been to reinforce how reliable rather than unreliable the later tradition was. With regard to the New Testament, the Dead Sea scrolls have thrown some most valuable new light on the background of contemporary Judaism *out* of which Christianity emerged. But the idea that they have upset all our previous ideas or forced us to revise our entire picture of Jesus is utterly wide of the mark. As regards the text and translation of the New Testament, I can remember one word in the Acts of the Apostles, used to describe the company of believers, which as translators of the NEB we considered *might* be more of a technical term than had previously been thought. But even this did not in the end alter the translation or even merit a marginal variant. So the revolution can hardly be said to have been shattering!

To return to the textual transmission of the New Testament, the wealth of manuscripts, and above all the narrow interval of time between the writing and the earliest extant copies, make it by far the best attested text of any ancient writing in the world. In the case of Greek and Latin classical literature it is not at all uncommon for there to be two or three manuscripts only and a gap of anything up to a thousand years. In the case of the New Testament there are, as I said, literally hundreds of witnesses, and in no case is the interval more than three hundred years and in many parts now a good deal less. In fact one papyrus fragment of St John's Gospel stands so close to the time of writing as actually to have ruled out some of the later (and in any case wilder) dates proposed for its composition. Besides this there is the indirect evidence of quotations in the early Christian Fathers and of versions in other languages (like Syriac, Coptic and Latin) which were taken from earlier texts now lost to us. So the statement of that professor of modern history that 'no Gospel text can be traced back even indirectly beyond the fourth century AD' is palpably wrong.

This does not, of course, mean that we know precisely what the New Testament writers penned. The very wealth of evidence makes the sifting and sorting out of it a most complex task. But two things can be said. When everything has been taken into account, the number of variants that make any difference (let alone any important difference) to the *meaning* is extremely small. The English reader may test this for himself by looking at the marginal readings at the foot of the page in the NEB. (They were unfortunately omitted in the popular, in contrast with the library, edition of the New Testament when that was first published separately, but they are there in the standard edition of the whole Bible.) There are two kinds of marginal readings, which represent possible, though not in the opinion of the majority probable, alternatives. One is introduced by a simple *'Or'* and that indicates a different way of translating the same Greek text. The other is introduced by a phrase like *'Some witnesses read* (or *add* or *omit*)'. This indicates an alternative manuscript reading, and is alone relevant for assessing the difference which textual uncertainty introduces. Going through these latter will show how relatively rarely the meaning is affected. Thus in the book of Revelation (which no scholar, incidentally, would ever call 'Revelations': where *does* this popular usage come from?) these can be counted on the fingers of two hands, and none seriously alters the sense.

The other thing that needs to be said is that almost certainly the original reading is in the vast majority of cases to be found *somewhere* in the existing manuscript tradition. In other words it has not been lost, so that we are left to guess or conjecture what it might have been. This is quite a different situation from that in many classical texts, where in the plays of Aeschylus, for instance, one of the main tests of the originality and judgement of editors is their ability to conjecture what the author might have written, since at so many points our existing manuscripts are quite evidently corrupt. There is a real difference here even between the New Testament and the Old, where a glance again at the NEB margin will reveal notes like 'Probable reading; Hebrew obscure'. There is nothing of this in the New Testament.

There are of course places where scholars come up with guesses about what the author might have written, and they may be right. But, as it seems to me, only about two conjectures in the whole text of the New Testament are at all compelling, both, as it happens, in St John. The first is in John 3.25, where the NEB reads, without any marginal note, 'Some of John's disciples had fallen into a dispute *with Jews*'. The RSV, again without recording an alternative, prefers the reading '*with a Jew*'. Bentley, the great eighteenth-century classical scholar and notorious Master of Trinity College, Cambridge, suggested that the original, now lost, read '*with Jesus*'. This gives excellent sense—though no one can say that the meaning is much affected either way. Again in John 19.29 the NEB says of Jesus on the cross, 'They soaked a sponge with wine, fixed it on a javelin, and held it up to his lips'. The RSV, like all the other English versions, has 'put it on hyssop'. Now hyssop, the little herb marjoram, is totally useless for fixing a sponge to! What the NEB has done is to follow a reading which differs by only one syllable (HYSSO instead of HYSSOPO). It happens to occur in one, eleventh-century, Greek manuscript, though it is almost certainly there a clever conjectural correction. Yet I believe the NEB is right in supposing it is what the author of the Gospel meant to write. Whether he actually did write it we shall never know. We tend to assume that the autograph started perfect, but nothing of any length that I have ever written was without a slip of the pen! In fact I am inclined to think that on occasion St Paul would have been the first to correct what his best manuscripts make him say. For example, in Rom. 5.1, I suspect he intended to write, 'We have peace with God', but Tertius who took it down (see Rom. 16.22) may well have been responsible for the minute change, mishearing a long 'O' for a short, that now causes him to say, according to our best witnesses, 'Let us have peace with God'.

I have given these detailed illustrations partly to show again how little difference such variations make. There are however other places where it is a more important matter of judgement whether what is in the later manuscript tradition (incorporated in the AV) originally formed part of the true text or not. Here, first, are three examples of verses that all scholars would agree are no part of the original text because they are missing from the best and earliest manuscripts.

1. Matt. 6.13b, the doxology to the Lord's prayer: 'For thine is the kingdom and the power and the glory, for ever. Amen.' This was clearly read back into the text of Scripture from its early use in liturgy, from which we are familiar with it—though it is interesting that it only got into the English Prayer Book as late as its final revision in 1662.

2. Mark 16.9–20. These verses, describing Jesus's resurrection appearances, were evidently added subsequently (certainly not by Mark) from other early Christian records, because it was thought (I

suspect rightly) that the point at which the best texts of the Gospel break off (16.8) was too abrupt to be intended as the original ending. The NEB margin registers other attempts to meet the felt need.

3. John 7.53–8.11. This story, of the woman taken in adultery, is certainly no part of the Gospel of John (from whose style it differs markedly). It is a piece of floating tradition (in some manuscripts it turns up after Luke 21.38). But that does not mean it is inauthentic. In fact it was probably felt to be too difficult (because too permissive) a story to be included in one of the finished Gospels—yet too like Jesus to be thrown away.

Here are two instances where there is not such a clear case.

1. Luke 23.34, 'Father, forgive them; for they do not know what they do'. Again this 'hard saying' is almost certainly not invented by the Church. If anything is, it is surely the *ipsissima vox* of Jesus. Yet it is missing from important manuscripts. It could well have been cut out by those in the Church who did not feel so charitable towards the Jews!

2. Another doubtful passage is the so-called 'longer text' of the institution of the Eucharist in Luke 22.19b–20, with its addition of the words 'Do this in remembrance of me' and a further cup. Here it is probably a question of Luke or some subsequent scribe combining the liturgical traditions of different Christian centres, one of them being found also in Matthew and Mark, the other being like that cited by Paul in 1 Cor. 11.24f. Whether the second was added to or cut from the original text of Luke is a matter of very delicate judgement. On the New Testament panel of the NEB we decided after long discussion to omit it from the text (though I recall voting for it). The first edition of

the RSV similarly put it in the margin, but the second restored it to the text! Yet ultimately it is not so important whether it was part of the text of *Luke*. For it was certainly part of the oral tradition of Jesus's words in the early Church.

Finally, here is a glaring instance of words which certainly never formed part of the true text of the New Testament. In 1 John 5.8 we read, 'There are three witnesses, the Spirit, the water and the blood, and these three agree'. Someone later embroidered this to, 'There are three who bear witness on earth, the Spirit, the water and the blood, and these are one *in Christ Jesus; and there are three who bear witness in heaven, the Father, the Son and the Spirit.'* The words in italics occur in no ancient Greek manuscript and were correctly omitted by Erasmus from his pioneering modern edition of the Greek Testament in 1516. But when attacked for taking things out of Holy Writ he rashly wagered to restore them if anyone could produce a Greek manuscript with them in. A late one was found that did contain them, where they were translated *back* from Latin. So he agreed, and thence they got into the text used by the AV! But, lest anyone should carry away the idea that the text of the New Testament is settled by bets, one should say that this is a totally isolated example. And in the end everything comes out in the wash: you will not find a trace of the interpolated words even in the margin of the RSV or NEB. But it does raise the question of the AV.

MODERN TRANSLATIONS
At this point we reach the last link in the chain connecting us with the original words of Jesus. For not only was he first translated into Greek, but most of us depend on a translation of the Greek. Can we trust these translations?

The answer again is, overwhelmingly, Yes. The number of places where the translations are actually wrong is minute. But time and again modern versions follow a more reliable text, bring out the sense more accurately in the light of scholarly research, and above all communicate it in a language that makes it more meaningful for us. 'The conservatism of the committed' includes a strong investment in what Englishmen call the Authorised Version, Americans more accurately the King James Version. For it has never been authorised. In fact if I this time were to conduct a wager, I am prepared to bet that most of my readers, if asked where the title comes from, would point, if anywhere, to the words on the title-page: 'Authorised to be read in churches'. Yet if they actually look this up they will find that what it says is 'Appointed (that is, assigned or provided) to be read in churches'. And this was *altered* from the title-page of the earlier Bishops' Bible, which had 'Authorised and appointed to be read in churches'. So the 'Authorised' Version actually came to be called by the very word it omitted! In fact it simply acquired its authority by usage, and it took a long time to establish itself. In the 1662 Prayer Book, nearly sixty years later, not only were the Psalms still in the Coverdale version of the previous century but sentences from Scripture which the revisers themselves put in (like the 'comfortable words' in the Communion service) were not yet in the King James Version.

The AV is of course one of the priceless treasures of the English language and no one wishes to decry its beauties or see it lapse. It is however worth remarking how uneven a translation it is (King James's men worked largely as individuals, unlike subsequent revising panels). Its merits are usually judged on its purple passages—like 1 Cor. 13. But even this, the famous hymn to charity, shows how derivative and indeed arbitrary a translation it was: at least eighty per cent of the wording was taken over from Coverdale, and so far from 'charity' being the inspired original which modern versions have 'ruined' by substituting 'love', it was King James's men who went out of their way to change Coverdale's 'love' on this and practically no other occasion. But in between such great passages there are others where one wonders whether even those who translated it understood what they were writing: try for sense some of the obscurer parts of 2 Corinthians! It is questionable too whether much of it was good idiomatic English of any age. I doubt if any Englishman ever used either the phrase 'fire of coals' (John 18.18) or 'coals of fire' (Rom. 12.20) —except in the latter case now as a quotation from the AV. Both are crudely literal renderings of the Greek, which in turn are crudely literal renderings of the Hebrew idiom—the sort of work that in school would be heavily marked down as translation English. Or take Luke 21.21: 'Let not them that are in the countries enter thereinto' (i.e., though you would not know it, the city of Jerusalem). Now 'the countries' was never English for the countryside: it just happens that the Greek for 'countryside' is a plural noun—so down it went.

I am not the least meaning to disparage—merely to detach the reader from dependence on what for Bible-study is a very blunt instrument. For such is the attachment to the AV that many people still talk of it as though it were the original. (In fact when I was a student I remember fundamentalists who were highly suspicious if you went behind it to the Greek, just as there were Roman Catholics who took the same attitude to the Latin Vulgate). When the NEB came out people always were asking me, 'Why did you change that?' I found it difficult to convince them that we 'changed' nothing. We never started from the AV nor had it in mind at all. In fact it was probably easier for us to put it out of our minds (not that we tried to) than it would have been for any other group of Englishmen. For most of us had probably not consulted it in our scholarly work for years. Indeed when I tried to find a copy for quoting in the course of writing this, I couldn't find one in the house. I had to borrow from my neighbour!

From the point of view of trusting the New Testament, as opposed to reading the Bible 'as literature' (for which it was never 'designed'—despite the popular book of that title), I would urge you forthwith to equip yourself, if you don't have one, with any good modern translation. The American RSV and the English NEB have the authority behind them of official committees of the Churches. (For convenience I shall normally quote from one of these— though I shall often go straight to the Greek.) But there are others, like that of J. B. Phillips, *The Jerusalem Bible* or *Good News for Modern Man*, which have their individual freedoms and advantages. In the next chapter I shall be going on to speak of 'the tools of discrimination' with which the scholar tackles his critical task. The least the layman can do is to acquire and use the tool most accessible to him, a good translation in contemporary English—which is itself one of the most important end-products of that long and laborious process.

3

THE TOOLS OF DISCRIMINATION

How does a New Testament scholar set about sorting out 'What you can believe and what you can't?' I have put those last words in inverted commas because that is never how he himself would put it. He would want to ask, What does this story or this saying tell us? Perhaps it may turn out to tell us more about what the early Church was interested in than what Jesus is likely to have done or said—and be just as valuable and true for that. It may be important evidence for reconstructing the whole developing picture of first-century Christianity—which itself produced the Gospels. No more than the archaeologist will the biblical critic dimiss finds because they do not come from the most primitive strata.

But first let us look at some of the tools that he has available and which themselves have been fashioned and refined by patient and dedicated study.

TEXTUAL CRITICISM
There is first the tool of textual criticism, which we looked at in the last chapter and so need not spend much more time on now. As well as providing a general presumption of what manuscripts are likely to give the best and most ancient readings, this also enables him to ask in a particular case, How can

you explain the existing variations? Is one reading likely to be a correction, to ease what seemed to the copyist a difficulty? Is there any reason why this unusual choice of words or this hard saying should have been invented if it was not original? Is the longer reading an explanatory gloss or an expansion of a shorter one, or is the shorter one due to an accidental or even deliberate omission? Has the reading in one Gospel, originally distinct, been assimilated to the parallel passage in another, particularly in familiar sections where the scribe may unconsciously be harmonising the two versions? Or is the eccentric text just a mistake?

There are no cut and dried answers. As a general working rule one can say that the shorter reading is to be preferred to the longer (on the ground that things get added to Scripture more easily than omitted) and the harder to the easier (on the ground that the easier is more likely to be a correction than vice versa). One could illustrate the preference for the shorter—and also the tendency of the scribes to assimilate—by the Lord's Prayer. We have already mentioned the way in which the doxology later got tacked on to the version in Matthew (6.9–13). But if you look at the version in Luke (11.2–4), you will see at the bottom of the page in the NEB a variety of other manuscript readings which expand his shorter and simpler clauses, usually to bring them into line with Matthew's. The preference for the more difficult reading is well illustrated in Mark 1.2f, which runs in the NEB: 'In the prophet Isaiah it stands written: "Here is my herald whom I send on ahead of you, and he will prepare your way. A voice crying aloud in the wilderness, 'Prepare a way for the Lord; clear a straight path for him' " '. But the first half of the quotation ('Here is my herald ... prepare your way'), unlike the second, is not from Isaiah but from Malachi. Some knowledge-able scribe evidently spotted this and corrected it to: 'In the *prophets* it stands written'. This is the text followed by the AV. The RSV relegates this reading to the margin. The NEB thinks it so ob-viously secondary that it doesn't even bother to mention it.

Unfortunately, however, textual decisions are seldom as simple as that. A convincing case can often be made on both sides, as in the instance of the longer or shorter text of the Lukan version of the last supper I mentioned in the previous chapter. And when does the harder reading become *so* diffi-cult as to be incredible? A notable instance (of some theological importance) is to be seen in John 1.18. The best manuscripts, now strongly reinforced by the latest discovery of an early papyrus, instead of the familiar words, 'No one has seen God: the only-begotten *Son* who is in the bosom of the Father, he has made him known,' read 'the only-begotten *God*'. This is so difficult even to translate intelligibly (see the NEB margin) that, against the judgement of re-cent editors of the Greek New Testament, both the RSV (even in its second edition) and the NEB con-clude that what John really intended to say was 'only-begotten Son'. Scholars too will diverge in their assessment of whether to pay more attention to the weight of manuscript evidence (in this instance unusually one-sided) or to the reasons why in any particular case poorer manuscripts may have pre-served the better reading. In fact, for all the ac-cumulated wisdom and knowledge, the state of play in textual criticism is probably as fluid at the moment as it has been for some time. Yet this is a sign of the softening of old dogmatisms (as in many of the natural sciences) rather than of chaos. It is not a reason for giving up in despair.

But we must move on from textual to literary or source criticism. As its name implies, this is concerned with questions of authorship, date, literary sources and documentary relationships. In the Gospels in particular it seeks to study and explain the close similarity at many points between the first three—so-called the Synoptic Gospels because they 'look together' at the life of Christ with a sort of stereoscopic vision. There is too much verbal agreement between them for this to be coincidental or due merely to common oral tradition. Either they are using each other or they have written sources in common—or both.

The dominant hypothesis among New Testament scholars is that Mark is the first Gospel, used independently by Matthew and Luke, but that these latter also drew on a common source (consisting mainly of sayings rather than happenings) usually known by the symbol 'Q'—as well as each using sources of material distinctive to himself. This consensus has of late been challenged, though not I think shattered. Some retain the priority of Mark but believe that Luke used not a hypothetical 'Q' but Matthew. Others go back to putting Matthew first, with Mark second and Luke third, or with Luke second and Mark third, each one knowing and using his predecessors. There are even one or two scholars who would argue that Luke is the first Gospel. I mention this confused state of affairs not to go into the pros and cons but as a word of warning that what is usually taken to be one of the most assured of the 'agreed results' of Gospel criticism remains a hypothesis; and it is thoroughly healthy that all hypotheses should be re-examined and questioned from time to time. So far from concluding that there is such uncertainty that one may as well believe anything or nothing, the proper response, as in any science, is a reasoned reassessment and a chastened humility.

It is too early yet to say what will come out of the re-opening of the question. (Many would hardly even be aware that it is open.) I would guess that each of the theories has been too simple to account for all the evidence. The solution to the Synoptic problem will I suspect turn out to be more complex than any that puts the Gospels as we now have them in a simple line of temporal succession, with B using A, and C using B and/or A. I believe that all of them developed over much the same span of time, partly overlapping and interacting. Apart from their distinctive traditions, they incorporated two main streams of common material. These are (a) the so-called triple tradition (because it is shared in different parts by all three evangelists), which Mark, usually, I would judge, though not invariably, tends to preserve in its most primitive state, and (b) the double or 'Q' tradition drawn on by Matthew and Luke, where again one has to judge on the merits of each instance which has retained the more primitive version. The earliest form of a saying or story may therefore on this view be found in any of the three —or for that matter, as we shall see, in John. I shall illustrate this in the sample I take later to exemplify all the critical tools at work. But whether one operates with the hypothesis of a single overall priority or judges each case more individually, the object of the exercise is the same. It is to assess the material in its various strata so as to be able, like the archaeologist, to place it and get it to 'speak' to us about the developing tradition. If some piece of material bears marks of being more distant from source, that does not mean it is useless. It may have much to tell us about tendencies at work within the life of the church, which can then throw light on the history of other material. We can begin to see things 'in depth' and not on the surface only. It adds a new dimension to our vision and discrimination.

FORM CRITICISM

The tools of literary criticism are closely related to those which work, not on documents, their dependence and sources, but on the motivations in the life of the community which shaped and passed on the traditions. These are the tools of what, somewhat unhappily, I think, has come to be called 'form' criticism. The starting-point was an analysis of the forms that moulded the separate units of material, such as are strung together in St Mark's Gospel, before they were written down and began to be subject to the influence of literary processes. But the really significant thing was the kind of questions which the form-critics, who started their work in Germany after the first world war, came to ask of the material, whether in its oral or in its written state. These questions were not so much concerned with *who* wrote it or *where* he got it from but with the interests in the life of the growing Christian communities that made this material relevant to them and therefore conditioned the shape in which it was preserved and passed on. What, for instance, had it to say to the conflicts and controversies of the early Church with the main body of Judaism, or to resolving issues of doctrine and discipline that arose within the developing congregations, or to policy-decisions about the admission of Gentiles to the Church, or to the moral instruction of new converts, or to settling matters of worship and ministry, or to answering difficulties and objections such as the apparent delay in the Lord's return? To meet these and other needs, stories or sayings of Jesus were recalled, adapted or recreated to convey what the living Christ would say to his people *now* in their situations of suffering or perplexity. We see this process at work in the Epistles, as St Paul draws upon and interprets a word of the Lord to discern what he takes to be the mind of Christ (though, it is to be noted, when he does not have one he says so: he does not think to invent one). What the form-critics have enabled us to perceive is that the Gospels, just as much as the Epistles, are Church books and therefore sources *in the first instance* for *its* life and theology.

It was understandable in the first flush of excitement about the new light which asking these questions shed on the life of the Church that the conclusion should be drawn that the more the Gospels have to tell us about the early Church the less they have to tell us about Jesus. And some of these critics, like Bultmann and to a lesser extent his English disciples, have, as I said earlier, been in my judgement unwarrantably sceptical about the historical value of the tradition. This is indeed the reputation the form-critics have got themselves. I recall my own theological college principal, when giving me one of the more conservative and constructive of their works, saying: 'I wouldn't let everyone have this!'

Yet other scholars have shown that this need not be the effect at all. Jeremias, for instance, in his book *The Parables of Jesus* (a model of how a New Testament scholar applies the tools of his trade) uses these and other techniques to peel away the layers of development and, by discounting the tendencies and interests which these questions reveal, get back to what underlay them.

Let us watch this tool at work in the kind of questions he asks. For example, Did the early Church reapply the parables in which Jesus warned the

Jews of the religious crisis in which they stood so as to alert its *own* members to be ready for the second coming? Why not?—these stories were too good to waste on situations and audiences that were now past. Did they go over them so as to draw out point by point who stood for whom, as, for example, in Matt. 13.37–9: 'The sower of the good seed is the Son of Man. The field is the world; the good seed stands for the children of the Kingdom, the darnel for the children of the evil one. The enemy who sowed the darnel is the devil. The harvest is the end of time. The reapers are angels'? Naturally—the instruction of simple converts demanded it. Did they elaborate the stories to make additional points— even if this did introduce strange matter—e.g., in the parable of the great feast in Matt. 22.7: 'The king sent troops to kill those murderers and set their town on fire' (while the supper was getting cold!)? Did they fuse one story with another as they collected them—thus creating, for instance, the difficulty in Matt. 22.11–14 of why the man picked up off the streets was blamed for having no wedding garment? Did they add riders at the end of the parables to point the moral or morals—like the whole string of them in Luke 16.9–13 to explain away that very difficult story of the unjust steward? Again, of course they did—as preachers have ever since. But once we recognise these and other tendencies at work we can begin to make allowances for them. We can 'aim off' and so get closer to the mark as we seek to recover the original teaching and meaning of Jesus. Then we can reapply *that* teaching and meaning, rather than some secondary application of it, to our own situation.

Source and form criticism have provided valuable tools for assessing the traditions that have gone to the making of our Gospels. (We can use them too on

the Epistles, for the patterns of instruction they dis-
close reflect the same community interests.) But in
all this the evangelists themselves tended to take a
back seat. They have been in danger of being rele-
gated to scissors-and-paste men who pieced together
documentary sources or suppliers of the string on
which the beads shaped by the processes of oral tradition were arranged. But this is seriously to under-
rate them—even though the traditional picture
(still there in *Jesus Christ Superstar!*) of the individual Apostles sitting down to write their memoirs
has gone for good.

REDACTION CRITICISM

So, since the second world war, there has been a
further tendency, to focus on what has come to be
known, perhaps equally unfortunately, as 'redaction' criticism (if only because to the layman it
sounds like 'reduction'!). Once again we owe the
phrase to the Germans—abetted this time by the
Americans. It comes from the word 'redactor' (to be
distinguished in these nuclear days from 'reactor'),
meaning editor. This approach recognises that the
Gospel writers were considerable moulders of the
tradition in their own right—though there has been
a tendency to turn them into 'theologians' theologians' with depths and subtleties of editorial patterns they might have been hard pressed to recognise! Yet they were not thinking up these things in
the isolation of their studies. For they too were
spokesmen of Church communities.

Since we have illustrated the other two kinds of
criticism from the Synoptic Gospels, let us turn for
an example of this last to the Gospel of John. For
John is above all the evangelist who has set his
stamp upon everything he writes. It has been said
of him that he seems to be saying to us 'la tradition

c'est moi!'. Yet this Gospel as redaction criticism sees it is not the product of one old man reflecting upon the memories of his youth. He is an editor, using sources and traditions which have come down to him, but shaping and adapting them to the needs and questions of his comunity. Thus, it is envisaged by a recent writer, John's church (whoever *he* was) is going through a crisis: members of it have been publicly banned from the local Jewish synagogue for confessing Jesus as the Christ. So, drawing upon traditions from a 'book of signs', he writes up the story that we have in John 9, which describes how Jesus encouraged a blind man who had suffered a similar fate. The 'history' in the story is the history of the group at the end of the first century or whenever it was, not of Jesus's time; but the message is what he, Jesus, is saying to the Church.

Again in the first flush it seems to me that greatly inflated claims have been made for this method. It has tended in the direction of seeing the Gospels as all theology and no history (except in the secondary sense just mentioned). It can also be very subjective and hypothetical. You have to begin by supposing your local community thrown out of the synagogue (needless to say there is no actual evidence of this). The rest is reading back or reading in; and the significances found often reflect the ingenuity of the scholar as much as anything inescapably present in the material. Yet again the perspective can yield valuable insights. We are all able to see the way in which a powerful personality like St Paul's imposes itself on all he writes. We should not dream of interpreting a particular passage except through 'his' mind. So too there is a Markan message and a Lukan theology which colours even what they take over from others. Everything they write has to be viewed through that glass of vision.

By now it might be thought that the words and acts of Jesus must be pretty well irrecoverable: all we can speak about with any confidence is the Christ of the Church's faith and preaching. And this has been the conclusion of many. I believe it is a false conclusion. I shall be spelling this out in relation to some of the big New Testament questions in the chapters that follow (especially chapters 6 and 7). But it might perhaps be helpful to sum up this one by taking a specific passage and demonstrating what I have called these tools of discrimination in actual use. I hope it will show how they can yield judgements which are not just picking and choosing what *we* like. They can help us to discern with some objectivity what is likely to go back to Jesus and what is not. This does not, of course, mean that others would not come to contrary assessments. But at least it is not simply a matter of arguing about tastes.

I choose a passage which is in each of the first three Gospels, where clearly there is literary dependence of some sort, and which can therefore illustrate all the types of criticism that I have been describing. To follow the comparisons the reader will have to look at all three versions together, and for this an invaluable tool is a 'synopsis' of the Gospels which sets them out (or at any rate the first three) in parallel columns. There are various editions of these, but the easiest and simplest for the English reader is one called *Gospel Parallels*, based on the text of the RSV. So if you have this or can get hold of it, turn to the parable of the 'wicked husbandmen' (p. 142). If not, have open together, or put markers in your Bible at: Matt. 21.33–46; Mark 12.1–12; and Luke 20.9–19.

I have chosen this passage also because there is now an interesting 'fourth column' available in yet another version. This is in the Gospel of Thomas, an apocryphal gospel whose text only turned up in a major discovery made in Egypt about the same time as that of the Dead Sea scrolls in Palestine. This was of a whole library of Gnostic books. The Gnostics were heretical Christians from the second and third centuries AD whom we previously knew only through the 'refutations' of the orthodox. They believed in salvation by knowledge ('*gnosis*') brought from the supernatural world and communicated to a spiritual élite. One of the effects of this discovery has been to throw doubt on the claims of some scholars that the central New Testament message of a heavenly Redeemer was itself *derived* from Gnostic myths. It is becoming clear (or at any rate clearer) that these myths are speculative and mystical versions, and perversions, of the Christian preaching. They also show something else, well illustrated by this particular sample from the Gospel of Thomas, which in fact reveals remarkably little sign of Gnostic colouring. This is that traditions of the teaching of Jesus were preserved alongside our canonical Gospels for a long time. For this 'Gospel' (though it is really just a collection of sayings) dates from at least a hundred years after his death and yet appears to go back to a tradition independent of our Synoptic Gospels and to be at some points more primitive. (The question of its dependence or independence is a delicate judgement, and not all scholars would agree, but this I think is where the evidence is pointing.)

Since its text is not so readily available, I will give it in full:

He said: A good man had a vineyard. He gave it to husbandmen that they might work it, and he receive its fruit at their hand. He sent his servant, that the husbandmen might give him the fruit of the vineyard. They seized his servant, they beat him, and all but killed him. The servant came and told his master. His master said: Perhaps they did not know him. He sent another servant; the husbandmen beat the other also. Then the master sent his son. He said: Perhaps they will reverence my son. Those husbandmen, since they knew that he was the heir of the vineyard, seized him and killed him. He that hath ears, let him hear.

Clearly this is the same story as in our Gospels, and by comparing all four versions we may see the kind of things that happen to a story on the way. Let me simply draw attention to some of the more significant.

In the introduction to the parable ('A man planted a vineyard and let it out to tenants') Mark and Matthew have the words 'and set a hedge around it and dug a pit for the wine press, and built a tower', but Luke and Thomas do not. They are details that are irrelevant to the rest of the story and are derived from and are clearly intended to echo the similar parable in Isa. 5.1–7. Since the details depend at one point on the Septuagint translation rather than the original Hebrew, it is improbable that they go back to the story as Jesus told it. They are evidently added to reinforce the point to the reader that 'the vineyard of the Lord of hosts' stands, as in Isaiah, for 'the house of Israel' and to stress the loving care of God for it.

Now the very fact that for the Christians telling it the story is still about the history of Israel and is a warning addressed by Jesus to the Jewish leaders (as they themselves well recognised) is significant. For the *form* of this story (of a man going away, delegating responsibility and requiring the fruits of it on his return) is repeated in several of Jesus's parables—of the servant entrusted with supervision (Matt. 24.45–51; Luke 12.42–6), the ten virgins (Matt. 25.1–13), the talents or pounds (Matt. 25.14–30; Luke 19.12–27), the door-keeper (Mark 13.33–7; Luke 12.35–8). In every other case it is applied not to the old Israel but to the Church, to warn it to be ready for the return of Christ. So if the Church made up this story we should expect its point to be the same. We may therefore have good confidence that it goes back to Jesus, and (unlike the others) is in its original setting. Nor in the Synoptic Gospels (in contrast with the Gospel of Thomas) has its context been lost by its becoming part of a collection of parables, such as we find, for the Church's teaching purposes, in Mark 4 and Matt. 13. In Mark and Luke it stands by itself (though Matthew has put other parables round it) towards the close of Jesus's ministry as a final and most explicit challenge to the Jewish leaders to accept him as the one whom God was sending to them.

But before him in the story others are sent, and there is a good deal of minor variation in the number of servants sent and in the treatment accorded to them. In his book *The Parables of the Kingdom* C. H. Dodd suggested that the oldest and simplest version was the typical triad of the folk-tale, of two servants followed by a son, who alone gets killed. He lived to see his suggestion vindicated by the Gospel of Thomas, which has precisely this. The rest of the detail is expansion and elaboration to bring the story more closely into line with the long list of Old Testament prophets and their fates (who are clearly those whom the servants are meant to represent). This is most obviously the case in Matthew's version, where the individual servants have been replaced by two waves, the second more numerous than the first, corresponding to the former and the latter prophets. This is a typical example of the process of allegorisation (making each of the details of the parable symbolic), which is especially characteristic of Matthew (compare, for instance, Matt. 13.37–43 and 49f).

It is the more surprising and significant therefore that at the next and most critical point, the sending of the son, which is the climax of the story, Matthew has the *least* allegorised version. He—and again Thomas—simply have: 'Afterward he sent his son to them'. Mark has: 'He had still one other, a beloved son; finally he sent him to them'. This carries just those marks of development that we might expect in the Christian tradition—the stress on uniqueness and finality and the epithet 'beloved', which is used of Jesus by the divine voice in the accounts of his baptism and transfiguration. They are descriptions not of the son in the story (they add nothing to it) but of the Son in Christian reflection. Nevertheless, the fact that he is a son and not just another servant is integral to the story in all its versions. It is difficult to escape the conclusion that Jesus was referring by this analogy from human life to himself and his relationship to God. *This* claim is not created by the Church. What the Church does is to expound and expand it. And the version that does this most explicitly is Mark's—who used to be thought the least theological! It is significant that Matthew, with Thomas, looks at this point to be nearest to source—though at other points, perhaps at most other points, he seems furthest away. It suggests, as I said earlier, that the hypothesis of a simple overall priority will not fit all the facts.

In what follows in the story, the fate meted out to the son, Mark has 'So they seized him and killed him and flung him out of the vineyard'. Matthew and Luke both have these events in the reverse order: he is flung out of the vineyard and then killed. A minor point perhaps, yet it is to be noted that this corresponds more exactly with what happened to Jesus, who was led away to be crucified *outside* the city. The change may therefore reflect later Christian tradition, though it is to be observed that it is *not* Matthew and Luke who make this point in their passion narratives but John (19.17)—and the Epistle to the Hebrews (13.12). So it is precarious to read too much theological motivation into what the evangelists are doing.

The climax of the story in the Synoptists is that the vineyard is taken away and given to others, and Matthew once more makes quite explicit by his allegorisation that the reference is to the Gentiles: 'The kingdom of God will be taken away from you and given to a nation that yields the proper fruit'. Thomas has no such point—only the stock warning, with which he rounds off many of his parables: 'He that hath ears, let him hear'. It is probable that, as so often, the application of the parable is secondary in all the versions. Jesus usually seems to have left his hearers to draw their own conclusion.

Finally, in all the Synoptic Gospels, though not again in Thomas, the parable is fused with an appeal to Scripture: 'Have you not read this scripture: "The very stone which the builders rejected has become the head of the corner"?' This is no part of the story proper, which ends with the son's rejection, not with his vindication. It may have been brought in to give the story a 'Christian' ending, with a veiled reference to the resurrection. Yet it has been pointed out that there is a concealed pun in the Hebrew between son (*ben*) and stone (*eben*)— and this challenging use of Scripture (in contrast with its confirmatory use by the evangelists to fulfil prophecies) is characteristic of Jesus. Moreover, the 'stone' saying forms the *next*, though separate, saying in the Gospel of Thomas—whose order does not elsewhere follow our Gospels. So there could well be a link that goes back to Jesus or early tradition, though the version underlying the Synoptists may have *fused* it with the parable.

What emerges? We may be pretty sure that we have here a story that comes from Jesus's own lips and carries the same point that he made. Yet in all sorts of small ways (from which I have merely selected) we can see how it was expanded and adapted to the Church's later use. The precision-tools which scholars have devised and refined enable us to discriminate with reasonable confidence and objectivity. Taken with a host of other examples, they can help us first to break down and then to build up. Disagreements there will be, because the presuppositions of those using the tools make a great deal of difference to the results. But that is a reason for getting together and pressing on, not for giving up. Technical difficulties too there are here, as in every other field of study. But that is not an argument for the layman to throw in the sponge: it is a challenge both to communication and to application. There is no reason why at a popular level it should be more beyond him than most do-it-yourself activities—or, say, the serious appreciation of music. And we do not regard music critics as threats, or as remote academics whose language it is not worth trying to learn. If even at second hand we can follow them, our understanding and perception will be enriched.

4

THE GENERATION GAP

WE have now looked at some of the processes which the tradition about Jesus went through and how scholars detect these and can to some extent play the tape back. But how extended was the tape? In principle it does not matter, but in practice it makes a considerable difference to our confidence in filling in the gap between the event and the records. What of those 'gulfs of oblivious mythopaeic time' in which anything could have happened and no one would have been any the wiser? Or, to change the analogy, the interval between the ministry of Jesus and the first written record of it has been described as a tunnel-period. Is there any means of checking that the train that went into the tunnel is recognisably the same as the train that came out? If there was no one around when the records came to be written who had been present at the events or had even heard their parents or grandparents talk about them, then obviously our controls are very much less direct. In fact trust in the New Testament documents for telling us anything about Jesus or the Apostolic Church has varied in inverse proportion to the distance from them at which the documents have been dated.

When was the New Testament written? The layman could be forgiven for expecting that by now the scholars might have settled such an elementary question. Yet the time-span over which the New

Testament documents have been held to come into being has expanded and contracted in concertina fashion—or rather having been stretched to its greatest lengths by the extremer German critics of the nineteenth century it has been contracting fairly steadily ever since. At the turn of this century, the span extended from about AD 50 to about AD 150—and that was already a good deal shorter than it had been on some reckonings. By the middle of this century, with the isolated exception of one book, it was halved, from about AD 50 to about AD 100. I am personally of the opinion that it should be halved, or more than halved, again, from about AD 47 to just before AD 70. I am well aware that this is an extreme position and I am compelled at this point to refer for the scholarly basis of it to a recent book of mine, *Redating the New Testament*. I merely give a summary of its arguments here. The reader should be warned that most New Testament scholars would not agree with me. But I believe that it represents the direction in which things are moving and I am convinced that the current critical orthodoxy reflected in the textbooks rests on far less solid evidence than the consensus would suggest.

A similar sort of revolution has been going on in prehistoric archaeology, and comparisons are instructive. Radio-carbon 14 dating and the modifications of this introduced by the evidence of tree-rings and in particular those of the incredibly long-lived Californian bristle-cone pine (the story is well told in Colin Renfrew's *Before Civilisation*) have very much upset the picture. Not only have they affected the overall span—in this case stretched it, so that monuments like Stonehenge are quite a lot older than was previously supposed. Much more significantly, they have confounded the assumptions on which the patterns of distribution, dependence and diffusion were so confidently based. For example, it was assumed that the megaliths of Brittany and Ireland (and the ideas and skills needed to build them) *must* have spread by diffusion from a single source in the Near East, whereas the datings now demonstrate that they were earlier and came into being independently. So many of the arguments about relative datings have been shown to be circular. Insert a new set of assumptions and another equally consistent pattern can emerge—with the intervals expanding or contracting according to the time available. It shows how much of what appears an established scholarly consensus rests not on hard facts but on the presuppositions by which they are interpreted.

Nothing so world-shattering or mind-expanding is happening on the much smaller scale of New Testament chronology. But I could not give my own answer to the question, Can we trust the New Testament?, without querying some of the reigning assumptions of the critics. For, as in archaeology, the number of firm absolute dates is far smaller than might be imagined: the rest, with the relative intervals and interconnections, have to be filled in by inference and deduction.

Here are some of the fixed points that are generally agreed:

AD 30	the crucifixion (possibly, but less probably, 29 or 33)
51–2	Gallio pro-consul of Achaia (Acts 18.12)
68	the death of Nero
70	the capture of Jerusalem by the Romans.

The Gallio date depends on the lucky accident of a

discovery of an inscription at Delphi published in 1905. A key date for which it would be most helpful if we had equally firm evidence is when Festus succeeded Felix as procurator of Judaea (Acts 24.27), for this would give us an end-term for Paul's missionary career and journey to Rome. But unfortunately, and rather surprisingly, we have not. Nevertheless, we can build in the basis of the intervals supplied at first hand by Paul himself in Gal. 1.18 and 2.1 (whose evidence is excellent but whose interpretation is much disputed) and by the author of Acts (who is very thin and vague at some points but very detailed and trustworthy at others, especially when, from the 'we' in the narrative, he himself was in all probability present). From these and other sources we may infer that the Council of Jerusalem described in Acts 15 took place about 48 and that Paul finally reached Rome, as a prisoner, about 60.

THE EPISTLES AND APOCALYPSE

Paul's letters roughly occupy the 50s. The earliest are probably 1 and 2 Thessalonians (50–1), followed by 1 Corinthians (55), 2 Corinthians and Galatians (56) and Romans (57), though some would put Galatians before the Council of Jerusalem in 48. Others would put the 'captivity epistles' (Philippians, Colossians and Philemon, and, if it is Pauline, Ephesians) up to a couple of years later, during his imprisonment in Rome (60–2) described in Acts 28.16–31. But I am convinced that they fit better into his earlier detention at Caesarea (57–9) described in Acts 24.22–7. The same applies, I now think (though this would not be generally accepted), to 2 Timothy, where the mention in 4.16 of 'the first hearing of my case' refers, I believe, not to some hypothetical trial (and subsequent release) in

Rome, but to that under Felix in Acts 21–4. In fact I am persuaded that the other two Pastoral Epistles, 1 Timothy and Titus—whether Paul himself actually penned them or had them written on his behalf —can also be fitted in earlier still, before he was in prison. This again would usually be denied (in fact many would put them years after his death, with genuine fragments possibly incorporated). But with regard to the main body of the Pauline Epistles there is not much difference of opinion. The value of thus being able to date at any rate the major Epistles with considerable confidence between 50 and 60 is that it supplies an absolute scale against which to measure other developments. It also shows how much can happen in a decade.

For the rest of the New Testament writings it will be convenient to consider them with reference to the two further landmarks mentioned earlier, one at each end of the Roman Empire—the death of Nero in 68 and the fall of Jerusalem in 70.

The death of Nero had been preceded in July 64 by the fire of Rome, which Tacitus, the Roman historian, tells us led to Nero fastening on the Christians as scapegoats after failing to allay the rumours that he himself had started it. Since he had by then already planned and begun the rebuilding of Rome, including a stupendous palace for himself, we can hardly put this persecution earlier than 65. If 1 Peter comes from the apostle Peter (and the reasons for doubting this are to my mind not compelling), then it looks from references to 'the fiery ordeal that is upon you' (4.12) as if it dates from the beginnings of that persecution. For I would agree with those who think that the allusions in the Epistle are best explained by the hypothesis that the material was originally prepared as sermon material for a congregation *in Rome* (perhaps at an Easter baptism), before, under the pressure of events, it was hastily converted into a letter (by the addition of 1.1f and 5.12–14) and sent off to Asia Minor. If so we could date 1 Peter with a fair degree of accuracy in the spring of 65.

2 Peter and Jude (which are clearly interconnected, since most of the material is reproduced in similar words and in the same order in 2 Peter) are much more problematic and frankly not very important. I treat them briefly here so as to get them out of the way. 2 Peter has survived as the one New Testament document still thought to have been written in the middle of the second century (under the false name of the Apostle). But the grounds for putting it so late appear to me a great deal less than compelling. I would completely agree that it cannot, on stylistic ground, be attributed to the same hand as 1 Peter. But I am not at all sure that it could not have been written during the Apostle's lifetime, by an agent on his behalf, as a final testament and reminder of the fundamentals of the faith to the churches of Asia Minor shortly before his departure for Rome. Perhaps indeed we can actually name the agent. For Jude describes how he has been forced to interrupt a longer letter to send an urgent appeal to the same readers to unite in the defence of the faith against false teachers (Jude 3). I suggest that that letter was 2 Peter, and that the earlier one on the same topic to which he refers in 2 Pet. 3.1 is not our 1 Peter (whose recipients and theme are very different) but that which Jude had written to them under his own name. For the style and much of the material are identical. In this case there would be no good reason for rejecting Jude's claim to be the brother of James, the Lord's brother (who, after all, would want to pretend to be Jude?), and to date the Epistles of Jude and 2 Peter before

James's martyrdom in 62: for they breathe no hint of persecution, in marked contrast with 1 Peter.

In any case it is this same James who is evidently claiming to be the author of the Epistle of James—and the very fact that he in no way flaunts his credentials as the brother of Jesus or as leader of the Jerusalem Church suggests that he is no imposter. Whether he could personally have written it has been much disputed, largely on the ground of its good Greek. But the mounting evidence going to show that at all social levels Palestine, and especially Galilee and Jerusalem, was bilingual makes this objection look less cogent than it did. Unlike the Epistles of Jude and 2 Peter, which belong to the 'silver age' of the early Church, the Epistle of James has a very primitive air about it. There appears to be no antagonism or even division between the Church and the Synagogue, all Christians, from its opening address in James 1.1, being assumed to be Jews. It shows no signs of developed Christian doctrine or Church order or of the arguments, such as mark the Epistles of Paul, about the terms on which Gentiles could be full members of the Church. It therefore seems to fit best *before* the great crisis which led to the Council of Jerusalem, when, we read, 'certain persons who had come down from Judaea began to teach the brotherhood that those who were not circumcised in accordance with Mosaic practice could not be saved' (Acts 15.1). Indeed these people may have claimed that they were drawing this 'all or nothing' implication from what James himself had written (cf. James 2.10: 'If a man keeps the whole law apart from one single point, he is guilty of breaking all of it'): hence the need for an official disclaimer from him and the Council (Acts 15.24). In this case the Epistle is likely to have been written not long before, perhaps in about 47. It would then be the first finished piece of Christian writing to have survived.

But to return now to the events arising out of the persecution under Nero. I believe that two more New Testament writings make best sense in this context. The first is the Epistle to the Hebrews, which is certainly not by Paul (despite its heading in the AV) and never claims to be: its style and thought-forms are decisively different. This is regularly dated by the textbooks round about 80–90—a decade convenient as a depository because we know remarkably little about it. But of all the books in the New Testament it would seem to me the *least* likely to come from after the destruction of Jerusalem and with it the end of the levitical high priesthood and the sacrificial system based on the temple. The author's elaborate argument, that this entire order of things must 'shortly disappear' (8.13), would have been pointless if it all at that moment lay in ruins. Indeed he says that 'the first tent' (representing for him the external structure of Judaism) 'still stands, ... which is symbolic of the present time' (9.8f). The letter I believe is clearly before 70. Yet those he addresses have evidently been through a good deal since they were 'newly enlightened' (10.32) and are in danger of relapsing under persecution that has already carried off their leaders (13.7). To cut a long story short, the Epistle to me makes best sense if sent to a synagogue of Jewish Christians in Rome who had lain low during the Neronian persecution, after the deaths of Peter and Paul (probably in 65–6) and yet before the relief brought by the suicide of Nero in 68—let us say, about the year 67.

The other work, in contrast, clearly reflects the rejoicing which this latter event brought for the Church. It is the book of Revelation. Usually this is dated about 95, but this dating rests ultimately upon one statement of the Church father Irenaeus at the end of the second century. Since he also thought it was written by John the apostle, this would make it the work of a nonagenarian, which is hardly probable. He was almost certainly wrong too in supposing it to be by the same author as the Gospel and Epistles of John, whose Greek style and cast of mind are markedly different. If we go to the book itself, we find that the seer interprets one of his visions of Rome with its seven kings by the words, 'Five have already fallen, one is now reigning, and the other has yet to come; when he does come he is only to last for a little while' (17.10). This like most of his symbolism is deliberately opaque, but the sixth Roman emperor was in fact Galba, who reigned from June 68 to January 69, immediately after the death of Nero by his own sword. The allusion to this event in chapter 13 and to the expectation, confirmed as current at the time by the Roman historians Tacitus and Suetonius, that he would return (like Hitler he was too evil really to be believed dead) underline the seer's preoccupation with Nero, the letters of whose name in Hebrew (the language evidently in which this strange man thought, whatever his pidgin Greek) add up to the number of the Beast, 666 (13.18). A dating in 68–9 is reinforced by another vision in 11.1–13, of the old city of Jerusalem. It is still standing, and the worst that happens to it is that in an earthquake (*not* by enemy action) 'a tenth of the city fell'. If the whole lay in ruins and the smoke of its conflagration, like that predicted of 'Babylon' (Rome), had actually been seen, as it was in its capture in 70, it is surely incredible that it should not have been described in the vision. The great Cambridge triumvirate of English New Testament scholars of the last century, Lightfoot, Westcott and Hort, all thought that the book of Revelation came from the period of the Neronian persecution (not that of the Emperor Domitian in the 90s), and I believe they were right. Indeed historians are increasingly questioning whether there *was* any organised persecution of the Church under Domitian—as opposed to the picking off of prominent individuals, some of whom may have been Christians, for reasons of state. In fact at whatever date we put the book, the figure of the Beast and the almost total martyrdom of the Church in a universal blood-bath is an imaginary projection on to the last times. It is the business of apocalyptic not to describe but to descry. The actual situation depicted in the letters to the seven churches of Asia Minor in chapters 1–3 reflects what need be no more than sporadic Jewish persecution—with but one martyr so far to show (2.13). Yet the frightfulness of the Neronian terror as described by Tacitus could have been sufficient to trigger off anything in the seer's imagination:

> An immense multitude was convicted, not so much of the crime of arson, as of hatred of the human race. Mockery of every sort was added to their death. Covered with the skins of beasts they were torn by dogs and perished, or were nailed to crosses, or were doomed to the flames. These served to illuminate the night when daylight failed.

ACTS AND THE SYNOPTIC GOSPELS

One of the most remarkable facts about the Acts of the Apostles is that it never mentions this terrible event (which from its excesses won, as Tacitus says, a good deal of sympathy for Christians). Nor does it record the deaths of Peter and Paul, or the outcome of the latter's trial—to which it has been leading up for many chapters. Nor does it confirm the fall of Jerusalem, which Luke's own Gospel is the most explicit in predicting (Luke–Acts being of course by the same author). Various explanations have been offered—including the guess that Luke was projecting a third volume. This is totally unsupported—and even so why should he have broken off volume two where he did? By far the simplest explanation is that Acts finishes where it does because this is where things had reached by the time it was written, two years after Paul's arrival in Rome—that is, about 62. In fact (and this is strongly supported by the Roman historian Sherwin-White whom I mentioned earlier) Acts accurately reflects the conditions of Roman society and Roman law at this very period (and not any later developments), and I am convinced that this is the date of the book.

However this has not been taken seriously by most critics (the great German historian of early Christian literature Harnack was a notable exception). For, it is said, Acts presupposes the Gospel of Luke (Acts 1.1), and Luke presupposes Mark, and Mark is generally dated about 65. The Gospels of Luke and Matthew are usually put well after the fall of Jerusalem—80–90 being again a favourite depository. The main grounds for these judgements are (a) that Mark, according to tradition, represents, in part at last, the committal to writing of Peter's preaching in Rome, and such a record would be more likely to be needed after his death (in fact one version of the tradition puts it after his 'departure' —though whether from life or from Rome is uncertain—but others say just the opposite); and (b) that Luke and Matthew, if not Mark, clearly reflect the siege and destruction of Jerusalem, which they present, after the event, as prophecies on the lips of Jesus.

How much weight we should in any case attach to the tradition that Mark depends on the preaching of Peter is debatable. I should be inclined to trust it, though to regard the connection with Mark's Gospel as we now have it as less direct. But in any case the dating of the Apostle's visit to Rome is quite uncertain. It is assumed to be at the end of his life, since he almost certainly died there, but Eusebius the Church historian, whose version is the only one to date the story, puts it during an earlier visit in the reign of the Emperor Claudius (AD 41–54) and indeed in the second year of that reign —and thus well before what would be required for an early dating of Acts. The first draft of St Mark's Gospel could be as early as 45.

With regard to the prophecies of the fall of Jerusalem, this is a matter of judgement. Are the details so precise as to require us to see them as composed in the light of the events? Most scholars have thought so in regard to Luke 19.43f, which has some very specific predictions of the siege and demolition of Jerusalem. In 21.20 too, Luke has in place of Mark's enigmatic phrase (derived from the book of Daniel), 'When you see "the abomination of desolation" usurping a place that is not his,' the words, 'When you see Jerusalem encircled by armies'. Again in 21.24 he has quite explicitly, 'They will fall at the sword's point; they will be carried captive into all countries; and Jerusalem will be trampled down by foreigners until their day has run its course'. These are generally taken as decisive evidence of prophecy by hindsight. But Dodd argued, conclusively in my opinion, that the details are derived *not* from what hapened in AD 70 (there is no mention, for instance, of the most unforgettable incident, the destruction of the temple by fire) but rather from Old Testament language about the capture of Jerusalem in 586 BC. Quite independently, the Swedish scholar Bo Reicke has recently come to precisely the same conclusion—and that not only for Luke but for Matthew as well.

In Matthew the most suspicious piece of evidence looks to be that in 22.7: 'The king was furious; he sent troops to kill those murderers and set their town on fire'. As we said earlier, this is clearly a most inappropriate addition to the parable of the great supper (it is not in Luke's version of the story), and it was evidently added by the Church against the Jews. The sole question is whether the correspondence is so exact as to require the addition to be *after* the event. I would doubt it. Jewish prophecies which were unquestionably composed after the event (like the book of Baruch in the Apocrypha or the Apocalypse known as 2 Baruch) go into much more precise detail, and if one really wants to see what such pseudo-prediction looks like, here is a Christian one from the so-called Sibylline Oracles: 'A Roman leader shall come to Syria, who shall burn down Jerusalem's temple with fire, and therewith slay many men, and shall waste the great land of the Jews'.

This is precisely the sort of detail that one does *not* get in the New Testament. Moreover, it is difficult to see what purpose would be served by perpetuating, let alone creating, such prophecies long after the dust had settled, except to show Jesus to have been a prognosticator of uncanny accuracy. But then why did Matthew and Luke also include such notoriously *unfulfilled* prophecies as these: 'Before you have gone through all the towns of Israel the Son of Man will have come' (Matt. 10.23); 'There are some standing here who will not taste of death before they have seen the Son of Man coming in his kingdom' (Matt. 16.28; Luke 9.27); 'I tell you the present generation will live to see it all' (Matt. 24.34; Luke 21.32). If their Gospels really do belong to the period 80–90, that is fifty to sixty years after the crucifixion, it is surely difficult to explain why modifications after the non-event did not also take place. Indeed, one of the few modifications—if that is the right way round to put it—Matthew made to the programme of the end in Mark 13 was actually to insert that the final coming of Christ would follow *'immediately* after' (Matt. 24.29; contrast Mark 13.24) the tribulation in Judaea (on this interpretation the war of 66–70). This scarcely suggests that he was deliberately writing for the period of delay between the fall of Jerusalem and the end of the world! It seems far more likely that, if (as the form-critics have taught us to expect) sayings of Jesus were pointed up to serve the uses of the Church, it should be when they were relevant to the struggle ahead, not when it was all over.

The other thing that the form-critics have rightly emphasised is that the Gospels are the product over a period of communities that collected and shaped material relevant to the needs of their developing life. This is not to deny the creative role of individual editors—particularly in the cases of Luke, who describes his own aim and methods (1.1–4), and John. But, unlike the Epistles, the Gospels were not written for specific occasions at a single moment of time. They appear to have grown from combining diverse traditions and to have passed through various stages and states. This I believe to be true of all the Gospels (it is quite likely, as many have thought, that Luke had already done a first draft of his Gospel before he came across Mark). But it is especially true of Matthew. The

Gospel of Matthew is in a sense a collector's piece, often holding together divergent traditions (e.g., about the coming of the Son of Man) which Luke has taken the trouble to harmonise. Matthew also has material with good claim to belong to the most primitive tradition of the Palestinian Church (and which has affinities with the Epistle of James and the early Paul) combined with quasi-legendary matter and editorial developments that appear to be among the latest elements in the Synoptic tradition.

All this adds up to the conclusion that the Synoptic Gospels grew up together over a period of time in different centres and varied contexts of the early Christian Church. They did not simply follow each other in a straight line of succession, but incorporated overlapping traditions, both oral and written, developing them, adding to them, and without doubt influencing one another. I should not wish to assign overall priority to any, though I would judge that in general Mark probably preserves the preaching tradition (based perhaps on summaries of Peter's) in its most primitive state, while Matthew and Luke will at differing points take us further back in the traditions of Jesus's teaching.

Where, however, I would differ from most New Testament critics is in doubting whether this extended process requires to be dated nearly so late as current orthodoxy would suggest. I believe the period 40–60 (which was also the creative period for the development of the Pauline preaching) satisfies the requirements well and that there is little or nothing that demands or suggests a later date—though developments in the liturgical and other life-processes of the Church naturally went on, which are reflected in the later textual tradition. But there is nothing, as I see it, in Mark or Luke which requires a setting later than the period of missionary expansion covered by the Acts story.

With regard to Matthew, his Gospel shows all the marks of being produced for a community, and by a community, that needed to formulate its own position over against the main body of Pharisaic and Sadducaic Judaism (the latter, the priestly party, virtually disappearing after the demise of the temple ritual in 70). It is concerned with such questions as the interpretation of Scripture and the place of the Law, its proper attitude towards the temple and its sacrifices, the sabbath, fasting and prayer, Jewish food laws and purification rites, its rules for admission and for the disciplining of offenders, for marriage and divorce, its policy towards Samaritans and Gentiles in a dominantly Jewish Church, and so on. These problems reflect a period when the requirements of co-existence compelled a clarification of what was the distinctively Christian line on a number of issues that could previously be taken for granted. This corresponds to the stage, in a later period of Church history, when the early Methodists in England were forced by events to cease regarding themselves simply as methodical Anglicans, loyal to the parish church and its structures as well as to their own class-meetings. At this point all kinds of questions of organisation, of ministry and liturgy, doctrine and discipline, law and finance, present themselves afresh, as a 'society' or 'synagogue' takes on the burden of becoming a 'church'. But uneasy co-existence does *not* imply irrevocable break: indeed John Wesley claimed that he lived and died a priest of the Church of England. It is in some such interval that the Gospel of Matthew seems most naturally to fit. This is well illustrated by Matthew's characteristic interest (in 17.24–7) in what should be the

Christian attitude to the half-shekel tax for the up-keep of the temple. The teaching of Jesus is taken to be that 'as we do not want to cause difficulty for these people' the tax should be paid, even though Christians may rightly consider themselves free. This certainly does not argue a situation of open breach, rather a concern not to provoke one. In any case it clearly points to a time before 70. For after that this tax had to be paid to the upkeep of a pagan temple in Rome and would have had no bearing on the *Jewish* question (not to be confused with the issue of the payment of tribute to Caesar raised in Mark 13.12–17) which Jesus is represented as settling.

If, therefore, we place the development and emergence of the Synoptic Gospels in the period up to 60 or soon after, it would narrow the gap between the crucifixion and the written records from some 35–70 years (on the usual reckoning) to little more than 30—with most of the material traceable a good deal further back. This would mean a gap of a single generation, comparable to the interval that now separates us from the end of the second world war. Of course legends can grow in that time (witness the angels of Mons even within the first world war), and much development and reflection can take place. But it would mean that the mists of 'mythopaeic time' are a great deal less impenetrable than the cynicism of the foolish—or even the scepticism of the wise—would suggest.

But there is still one significant part of the New Testament literature that we have not mentioned, the Gospel and Epistles of St John. How does this fit into the new picture? It was indeed from considerations forced upon me by the Fourth Gospel that I was originally compelled to look again at the old picture. To treat them in a separate chapter will also allow us to reassess the place of this Gospel to-day, which is, properly, of so much concern to the conservatism of the committed—not to mention the fundamentalism of the fearful.

5

JOHN'S PICTURE OF JESUS

For the past 150 years or so the Gospel of John has suffered from being isolated—almost insulated—from the others. Up to that time even so liberal a theologian as Schleiermacher could treat it on a par with the rest and indeed regard it as having priority for the picture it gave us of Jesus, since it was the one by the most intimate of his apostles. But over against the Synoptic Gospels John has been treated as the odd one out—in a minority of one to three, and doing quite a different job. In the hey-day of Liberal Protestant criticism, in the late nineteenth and early twentieth century, Mark supplied the Jesus of history, John the Christ of faith. From the historical point of view, John was entirely secondary, dependent on the Synoptists for anything reliable that he incorporates. In space and time too he was far removed from any direct, or even indirect, contact with the person whose significance it was his contribution to draw out in the categories of Hellenistic (that is, late Greek) mystical philosophy. In date he was put as late as AD 170. This last has at any rate been knocked out by the most direct piece of evidence possible, the discovery of an actual fragment of the Gospel dated by the palaeographers from the first half of the second century—and time must then be allowed for it to have been copied and reached Egypt, in whose dry sands it was preserved. But this was only the first blow to an assessment of the Gospel which has become more and more incredible over the years.

For one thing no one now believes in the simple view that Mark gives us the Jesus of history, John the Christ of faith. The tendency if anything is to believe that both give us the Christ of faith, with the Jesus of history a long way, perhaps irrecoverably, behind. That I am convinced is an exaggerated reaction. In fact it is becoming clear that Mark is much more theological and John much more historical than was previously supposed. It is also becoming clear that the consensus is rapidly dissolving that John is dependent upon the Synoptists (or, more precisely, that he certainly used Mark, probably Luke and possibly Matthew). This indeed has been one of the swiftest turn-abouts in critical history. For up to the publication twenty years ago of C. K. Barrett's valuable commentary on the Gospel of John he was in the great majority in holding this: now he is very much in the minority. John is increasingly seen to rest on independent tradition, which therefore, is *potentially* as near to source as any of the other streams of Gospel tradition (those represented in Mark, 'Q', special Matthew and special Luke) and must be considered alongside them as part of the total 'synoptic' or stereoscopic picture of Jesus. One of the decisive reinforcements of this trend was Dodd's major study, *Historical Tradition in the Fourth Gospel*. The effects of this shift and of other aspects of what I ventured, again nearly twenty years ago, to call 'the new look on the Fourth Gospel' (historians of women's fashion will be able to date it from 'the New Look'!) have been popularised in A. M. Hunter's *According to John*.

The upshot has been to suggest that at many points both in the narrative and in the sayings of Jesus, John preserves tradition with as good, and often, better claim to take us back to source as comparable material in the other Gospels. Moreover, even the language of John, which he puts into the mouth of Jesus, is now seen to be neither so Hellenistic nor so late as was previously thought necessary. One of the by-products of the Dead Sea scrolls was to reveal that similar language was being used in the heart of southern Palestine by a strictly nationalistic Jewish group before the destruction of Jerusalem. The Gospel of John is now once again being seen as the very Jewish book it is (Lightfoot called it the most Hebraic book in the New Testament apart from the Apocalypse). That does not mean that by then the 'mix' between Hellenistic and Hebraic cultures was not far advanced. Indeed the Gospel is written in correct but simple Greek, with what might be called an Aramaic accent. It is addressed in its present form primarily, I believe, to Greek-speaking Jews outside Palestine, probably in the area of Asia Minor around Ephesus. This location is borne out not only by good ancient tradition about John's presence in Ephesus but by the book of Revelation from the same area, which though almost certainly not from the same hand presupposes a 'Johannine' type of Christianity.

All this is not incompatible with a view that the Fourth Gospel preserves and incorporates early material about Jesus but is itself written quite late, by someone who himself stood in a distant and external relationship to that material. Indeed this is what Dodd presupposed. He thought of an Ephesian 'elder' in the last decade of the first century (the now generally favoured date) who wrote up traditions that 'came down to him'. *How* they came down to him is indeed a relevant question. Attempts to analyse out written sources behind the Fourth Gospel have not been conspicuously successful. In fact such is the stylistic uniformity of the book that I would agree with the American scholar who said that 'if John used sources, he wrote them all himself'! Dodd presupposed that the traditions came down to the evangelist by word of mouth—and yet in a form that time and again reveals them to be very 'primitive' and to carry the marks not of Asia Minor in the 90s but of Palestine before the Jewish war of 66–70. But what was this invisible medium through which they passed uncontaminated for a full generation?

Many attempts have been made to bridge the gulf between the original apostolic traditions (which could, it is agreed, well derive ultimately from John the son of Zebedee) and the evangelist and various redactors or revisers. There is no doubt that this Gospel, like the others, has passed through developing stages. For one thing, it is clear that the 'epilogue' of chapter 21 was added subsequently to the rounded close of 20.30f. I believe too that the prologue of 1.1–18 has been fitted on to, or rather round, the original opening, like a porch. There are other signs of editorial touches and revisions (and lack of revision)—though I am not persuaded that any of the additions demand a different hand (except of course the certificate appended by the Johannine community in 21.24: 'It is this same disciple who attests what has here been written. It is in fact he who wrote it and we know that his testimony is true'). What seems to me much more questionable is to say that the main body of the Gospel itself represents the remoulding after a long interval by some totally unknown spiritual genius of traditions that themselves bespeak the conditions of a much earlier age. I would merely wish to ask whether this time-span and with it the separation of the evangelist from his tradition is really necessary—especially in view of the scale of development for which I argued in the previous chapter.

The arguments for a late date for the Gospel of John may be summed up under three heads:

1. There is the ancient tradition that John wrote 'last of all', though this goes with the theory that his object was to supply information that the others left out, which is hardly a plausible view of their relationship. It is bound up too with the tradition, which is not in itself incredible, that the apostle John lived on to the very end of the first century, though the common notion that he *wrote* as a very old man is one for which the first evidence is quite late and unreliable. (In John 21.18 the old man is *not* the beloved disciple but Peter, who must have lived at most to his sixties.) But if what we have argued in the previous chapter is right, John's could still be the last Gospel and yet not be very late.

2. *If* he is dependent on the Synoptists and *if* these were written towards the end of the first century, then of course he must be later still. But neither of these 'ifs' seems to be necessary or indeed likely.

3. John is usually held to come out of a situation in which the Church and Synagogue have irreparably split (as in the reconstruction I mentioned earlier of the blind man thrown out of the synagogue) and to reflect a Jewish ban against the Nazarenes which came into force in the late 80s. But any connection with this ban (which was against extreme Judaising Christians to whom St John's Gospel would have been anathema, who did not

want to leave the synagogue and had to be 'smoked out') is very tenuous. Christians like Paul were already being thrown out of the synagogue much earlier. Indeed in 1 Thess. 2.14–16, in what is probably his earliest epistle, written about 50, Paul speaks in much the same external way as John does of 'the Jews' in Judaea who 'drove us out'. In neither case does this imply a final breach. Excommunication was such a common discipline—for instance, as we now know, in the Qumran community—that is is quite unreliable for dating.

For the rest we are dealing with developments of doctrine and language which *could* be late, but do not need to be later than anything, say, in Colossians and Hebrews, which equally speak of the pre-existence of the cosmic Christ but certainly, in my judgement, come from before the fall of Jerusalem. Indeed the Fourth Gospel, like the Epistle to the Hebrews, is a document where the argument would seem positively to invite allusion, however indirect (and John is a master of this), to the fall of Jerusalem and the destruction of the temple. Since the rejection of Jesus as the true Messiah, Shepherd and King of the Jews involves the inevitable judgement of metropolitan Judaism, the consummation of this in the doom of the capital could scarcely escape mention if it had occurred. Yet the only reference to it lies in the future, when in 11.48 the High Priest warns that if they do *not* do away with Jesus (and not, as actually occurred, if they do) the Romans will come and remove their temple and nation. The destruction of the temple, so far from being described physically in the light of events of 70, is seen as fulfilled spiritually in the death of Jesus in 30 (2.19–22). Nor is there any hint of later conditions being read back. In fact in 5.2 the evangelist observes, 'There *is* in Jerusalem at the Sheep-

Pool a place with five colonnades, called in Hebrew Bethesda'. This was to be obliterated in the demolition of the city, only to be uncovered and confirmed recently by the archaeologist's spade. Yet John says emphatically at the time of writing (and not just of Jesus's speaking) 'is' not 'was'. Moreover, his knowledge not only of the topography but of the unrepeatable social and political conditions of Palestine prior to the Jewish war has been borne out in recent study.

If then we reopen the question of the dating of this Gospel as of the others, what pointers are there to anything more precise? Working backwards, we may note what is almost certainly a reference in 21.18f to the death of Peter, which early tradition says was by crucifixion: 'You will stretch out your arms and a stranger will bind you fast.... He said this to indicate the manner of death by which Peter was to glorify God'. Peter met his death in all probability in the persecution of 65. Thereafter John was the last survivor of the 'pillars' of the apostolic Church mentioned in Gal. 2.9. James the Lord's brother had been killed by the Jews in 62, Peter and Paul had perished under Nero. It would not be surprising (and indeed it is amply confirmed by the book of Revelation if it comes from this date) if this quickened the expectation that the end must surely now come soon (cf. Rev. 22.20). A word of Jesus interpreted to mean that 'the beloved disciple' would live to see it was evidently being used in support—not because he was so old but because it was so imminent. It seems much more likely that this misleading interpretation should need to be corrected soon after Peter's death, with which it was associated, than some thirty years later. A date of writing therefore of 65+, still prior to the Jewish rebellion (of which there is no foreboding in the Jews' obsequious dealings with Pilate) and the fall of Jerusalem, would fit well for the final version of St John's Gospel.

But so far we have been dealing with the epilogue, which must be considered with the prologue, and this in turn has to be viewed alongside the Johannine Epistles. For they share the same concern to insist that Jesus Christ had really come *in the flesh* (John 1.14; 1 John 4.2; 2 John 7), and indeed the prologue to the first Epistle (1 John 1.1–4) reads almost like a preliminary sketch for that of the Gospel. The Epistles reflect the same danger to the Church from the sort of 'Gnosticising' Judaism that we meet, also in the Ephesus area, in Colossians, 1 Timothy and the letters to the churches in Rev. 1–3, and (probably also from Asia Minor) in Jude and 2 Peter; and there appears no reason why they should not come from the same period, round about the early 60s. They are written to recall the faithful to fundamentals from which they are in danger of being shaken by distortions of the message that they had had from 'the beginning'. It is clear that there has since been time for a good deal of water to have passed under the bridges and both heresy and schism have assumed menacing proportions. The message to which the readers are being recalled is clearly that enshrined in the Johannine tradition—and, allowing for the lapse of time and the change of perspective, I see no decisive grounds for not thinking the author of the Epistles and Gospel to be the same man. Since his purpose in writing the Gospel was evangelistic (John 20.31), it makes sense to assume that it was originally composed and used for this purpose. If so, then, in some form or other, it will go well back into the 50s, at any rate in Asia Minor.

But the tradition that makes it up shows every

sign of having taken shape in debate and controversy with Jews in the heart of Palestine. All the arguments are Jewish arguments and there is not even, as in Matthew (let alone Luke), a hint of the questions that arise from Gentiles pressing in upon the wings: there is not a non-Jew in the Gospel, except Pilate and his soldiers ('Am I a Jew?', he asks in scorn). Christ is indeed the saviour of the whole world. John's Gospel is the least exclusivist or nationalistic. But his object seems to be to present this universalistic gospel as the true fulfilment of Judaism: Jesus as the Christ, the King of the Jews, is the *real* manna, vine and shepherd of Israel. The problems arising from the terms on which *Gentiles* can enter and live in the Church do not seem to come within his purview. The children of God scattered abroad are still thought of in Jewish categories (7.35; 11.52). The 'Greeks' who come up to worship at the festival and ask to see Jesus (12.20f) are evidently Greek-speaking *Jews*. And this could well reflect the kind of missionary encounter centred on Jerusalem out of which the tradition of the Gospel was hammered. Indeed, I believe it is probable that it took shape, in Greek, out of dialogue with the Greek-speaking Jews of Jerusalem (of whom Nicodemus with his Greek name is a representative sample) even before it was carried to Asia Minor—though the first language of its author was almost certainly Aramaic.

If this is anything like its history (and the 'we' of the Johannine community is never far away to show it was much more than the work of one man, however dominant), then this Gospel tradition was coming to fruition simultaneously with the others —and doubtless in cross-fertilisation with them (hence some of the verbal parallels that have suggested literary dependence). It represents a tradition that basically took shape like the others in the 40s and 50s, though I believe its final stages reflect slightly later developments and events—hence the truth too in the report that it was written last. But though it is in so many ways the maturest of the Gospels, it can also take us just as far back—if not further—to source. And at this point we cannot finally escape the question of authorship.

The association of the Gospel with John the son of Zebedee is too strong simply to dismiss, but most scholars have found it impossible to see him as more than the source, or a source, of its tradition. It is also fairly widely (though by no means universally) accepted that 'the disciple whom Jesus loved' is *intended* to represent the apostle John (otherwise an unaccountable absentee from the Gospel, like his brother James), even if the claim of the Gospel itself is not accepted that 'it is in fact he who wrote it' (21.24). More important, ultimately, than who actually penned it is whether the tradition it represents does go back to source and whether the evangelist stood within that tradition rather than outside it (as even Dodd thought). I believe that the answer to both these questions should be, Yes. Having got that far, fairly cogent reasons have to be advanced that the author should *not* be John the son of Zebedee. One of the most powerful is that 'an ignorant Galilean fisherman' could not have written it. This objection begins to look less convincing with the evidence that his religious vocabulary is not necessarily so Hellenistic or so late, nor is his Greek style as cultured even as those of 1 Peter or James. Moreover, Zebedee, with his two sons and hired servants, is much more comparable with the father in the parable of the prodigal son, who was similarly placed and evidently a man of some limited substance, than an illiterate peasant, Indeed, if we are looking for a candidate who fits the requirements, we should have to go a long way to find another who knew both Galilee and southern Palestine intimately, was a leader of the apostolic mission in Jerusalem and Samaria (Acts 3–4; 8.14–25) and, as Paul tells us on the highest authority in Gal. 2.9, was one of the those who from Jerusalem undertook to 'go to the Jews'. To duplicate such characters, above all to invent a shadow who is a spiritual genius and theological giant, is scarcely a scientific procedure if there is any alternative. Against the stream of critical opinion, therefore, I am compelled to say that I have come to find apostolic authorship, within the context of an ongoing missionary community, the hypothesis which presents the least difficulties.

Now if we admit this we are very close to source indeed—within the innermost circle of the Twelve—and this has, of course, been the contention of those like Lightfoot and Westcott who argued strongly for the traditional authorship. But lest the conservative-minded should at this point jump to the conclusion that this means that we possess the equivalent of a video-tape or a photograph, it is important to emphasise at once that it means nothing of the sort. In fact to assume that *this* is the sort of truth the Gospel is giving us is to show a crass misunderstanding of its own claim.

THE TRUTH OF THE PICTURE

The claim of the evangelist is indeed that 'his witness is true' and the context in which it is made shows that this is not just 'spiritual' truth unrelated to physical fact. For in recording the death of Jesus he says: 'One of the soldiers stabbed his side with a lance, and at once there was a flow of blood and water. This is vouched for by an eye witness, whose evidence is to be trusted. He knows that he speaks the truth, so that you too may believe' (19.34f). It is the truth *of* the history of which he speaks—yet the purpose of his recording it is primarily in the interest of *faith* (that you may 'believe'), not of fact for its own sake. Moreover, water and blood have profound spiritual significance for this writer, as his reflection on these themes in the first Epistle makes clear (1 John 5.6–8). In fact John is at his most theological when he is most historical, and most historical when he is most theological. His purpose is to show the *Word* made *flesh* (1.14)— and the one is of equal importance with the other. His method is, as it were, to project two colour transparencies at once, one over the other. It is possible, like the Jews, to see only the one, as the eyes see (7.24), at the natural level (8.15), and so to miss or to misunderstand everything. Or it is possible to see only the other, as many Christian interpreters have done, and to regard the flesh as unreal, a transparent sham. (This was evidently an early reaction, as the writer has to come back on it in the Epistles and to insist, as in 2 John 7, that to deny the flesh of Jesus is nothing less than Antichrist.) But to see the 'glory' *in* the flesh is to know the truth that sets one free. And the verity of this is what John is interested in—not verisimilitude for its own sake. Judge the Jesus of this Gospel purely at the level of psychological analysis, and you will probably conclude, with the Jews, that he is a megalomaniac. For, in every sense, 'no man ever spoke like this man' (7.46). No sane person goes around saying 'Before Abraham was I am' (8.58) or 'Whoever eats my flesh and drinks my blood shall live for ever' (6.56–8). These are theological interpretations, not literal utterances. Yet at the deepest level of faith they may indeed be the truth about the eternal Word of life, made flesh in this supremely individual and uniquely normal man of history.

If we are not to misinterpret and therefore to *mis*trust John, it is vital to see what he is doing. So perhaps it may be helpful to end with a sample dip into his Gospel to illustrate the importance, and the profundity, of this.

The last quotation ('Whoever eats my flesh and drinks my blood shall live for ever') is taken from his sixth chapter, which on any count must be one of the most theological of all. In it he expounds the teaching of Jesus as the bread of life and it is on this rather than on an institution narrative at the last supper that he bases his profound interpretation of the Eucharist. We appear to be worlds away from 'the Jesus of history'. Yet this chapter begins (6.1–15) with a story that has many marks of very good historical tradition. It is the one miracle story —the feeding of the five thousand—reproduced in all four Gospels, and John's account is at points so close to the others as to provide one of the stronger arguments for literary dependence. Yet it is John alone who allows us to glimpse a dimension of this incident that is entirely obscured in the Synoptic accounts. Had we been looking for it we might have noticed in Mark's story the almost manic excitement of the crowds as they rush after Jesus in the desert (Mark 6.33). Or again we might have observed the significance of the fact that they are all males (6.44)—as they are also in Luke and John: Matthew's addition 'besides women and children', both here and in the duplicate story of the four thousand, seems to be a typical expansion of his to heighten the miraculous. Again there is the very curious ending when Jesus 'forces' the disciples to go off in a boat *before* he dismisses the crowd and withdraws to the hills (6.45f). But these things are suddenly lit up by the clue which John alone supplies: 'Jesus, aware that they meant to come and seize him to proclaim him king, withdrew again to the hills by himself' (John 6.15).

For behind this wilderness gathering was *not only* whatever physically this miracle of sharing involved, *not only* the mystical and sacramental truth which the Church came to see in it, but a highly charged political moment. For it very nearly turned into a para-military desert rising, leading to a messianic march on Jerusalem to overthrow the Romans. Josephus the Jewish historian records a number of such attempts, including that mentioned in Acts 21.38 of 'the Egyptian who started a revolt some time ago and led a force of four thousand terrorists into the wilds'. Doubtless many of the disciples too would have been glad to back this sort of liberation movement. Jesus evidently could not trust them: and shortly afterwards he found it necessary to test the terms of their loyalty to him (Mark 8.27–33; cf. John 6.66–71)—for reasons that the Synoptists never explain.

It is characteristic of John that he should make possible the greatest awareness not only of the spiritual but of the political dimension of Jesus's life and death. For not only in this crisis but supremely in the story of the trial he interprets more profoundly than anyone else, what it really did, and what it did not, mean for Jesus to be 'the King of the Jews'. Nowhere, as we shall see later, are the strands of the religious and the political charges against Jesus so intertwined, and also so carefully distinguished, as in John. One of the critical points in the interpretation of the New Testament today is the sifting of the claim, made by both Christians and non-Christians, that Jesus was a 'revolutionary', mixed up with Zealot aspirations to bring in the kingdom of God by force. Indeed it is interesting that 'the quest of the historical Jesus', to use the title of Albert Schweitzer's famous book (which was called in the original German 'From Reimarus to Wrede'), began with the attempt by a certain H. S. Reimarus in the eighteenth century to present Jesus in this way as 'the political Christ' (to use the title of a recent book by Alan Richardson, much to be recommended on this subject). It was due to this simplistic reading of the evidence that Christians and others were driven to the bar of history, where alone it could be tested— by better scholarship. That John should be vital evidence in *that* case shows how, if we can use (and again do not abuse) his testimony, it can take us, *alongside that of the others*, to the Jesus of history who remains an integral part of the Christ of faith.

For I would end where I began to pleading against the isolation of John in the treatment of the evidence. So, rather than close this chapter by trying to sum up *John's* picture of Jesus on its own, I should like it to lead into two other chapters that will look at what the New Testament as a whole, and not even the four Gospels alone, give us by way of answer to perhaps the two most fundamental questions it raises—'Who is this man?' and 'What came of him?' They are also test questions for how far and in what way we ourselves can trust the New Testament as a truthful record.

6

WHO IS THIS MAN?

FROM the opening chapter of the New Testament
onwards this is the question that is constantly being
posed. In fact the 'prologues' to all the Gospels in
their different ways represent answers to it. It is a
deeply theological question, and even the simplest
and shortest of them, that of Mark, packs an enormous amount into one verse: 'The Gospel of Jesus
Christ the Son of God' (1.1). The others are all
elaborations of this in different directions.

WHERE IS HE FROM?

Matthew and Luke do it by telling the story of
Jesus's ancestry and birth. But this is not done with
the interest that a modern biographer might have
in what made his hero genetically and culturally
the sort of person he was, or because it is a beautiful
story in its own right. Almost all the things in it—
the symbolism, the scriptural overtones and quotations, even the place-names—are there to answer
the theological question: Who is this man? In fact
Matthew concentrates on drawing out the significance of the first of Mark's titles, 'Jesus Christ',
Luke on that of the second, 'the Son of God'. How,
Matthew asks with an eye to Jewish objections and
slanders, can Jesus be the Messiah of Israel, when,
apparently, he comes of an irregular union (thus
breaking a fundamental requirement of the Law)
or from Nazareth and not Bethlehem (where as

David's son the Messiah should be born)? So in his first two chapters he proceeds to give the Christian answer to these questions. Despite the irregular union Jesus's birth *is* the work of the Spirit of God, for God has used irregular unions before to further the Messianic line (this is the point of the four women in Matthew's genealogy). Again, despite Nazareth being his *home*-town, Jesus was actually *born* in Bethlehem, and was, by Joseph giving him his name, engrafted into David's line. Similarly, Luke shows in two ways how Jesus is 'Son of God'. The divine initiative in his annunciation and conception reveals him to be the son, not simply of his human parents (which Mary and Joseph are called), but of God. Secondly, Luke's genealogy goes back further than Matthew's, to declare him not only son of David and son of Abraham but 'son of Adam, son of God'.

The centre of interest of the new 'book of Genesis' (the opening phrase of Matthew in the Greek) is not gynaecology, any more than that of the old one is geology. To search it for answers to such questions or to take the stories at that level is to misread them. The descriptive details are often supplied by the Old Testament. There is obviously, for instance, a close parallel between the Magnificat in Luke 1.46–55 and the Song of Hannah in 1 Sam. 2.1–10. Matthew in particular is concerned to show how everything is a fulfilment of what God has been up to from the beginning, bearing throughout the watermark of his signature. (This is brought out strongly in the popular book by the Roman Catholic Hubert J. Richards, *The First Christmas* —though he tends perhaps to see it everywhere.) Whatever the underlying history (and there is no reason to suppose that there is not quite a lot of history, particularly in Luke), it is overlaid and interpreted by stories with all the legendary and mythical beauty of folk-tales—whose point is not to distract *from* the history, nor again to be taken simply *as* history, but to draw out the divine significance *of* the history. Once we forget this and start asking prosaic or scientific How? questions rather than meaningful or interpretative Why? questions (whether of the opening chapters of the Old Testament or the New), then not only do we miss the point for ourselves: we put stumbling-blocks in the way of other people. By asking them to credit the entire infancy narrative (stopping stars and all) literally as history we are in danger of *dis*crediting it. For that is not what is was 'written up' to be. I have no doubt, as I said, that there is history behind it, and as a New Testament scholar I am interested in digging into this (even into the possible relevance of comets for determining the date of Jesus's birth). But that is not the point. Doubtless there is some history behind the story of the Flood, but to send expeditions looking for arks on Ararat is not the way to bring home the real truth of that story. So too the marvellous stories of the annunciation and the virgin birth, the wise men and the shepherds, the massacre of the innocents and the flight into Egypt, may indeed reflect fact. But to take it all, with the fundamentalists, as prose rather than poetry is to confound everything, and, these days, to put off a large number of intelligent people.

The point of these two prologues, told in picture-story form, is in fact the same as that of the last, St John's, told in another form of poetry—namely that the life of Jesus, and indeed the life of Christians as children of God, is not to be explained *simply* in terms of 'human stock or the fleshly desire of a human father' (John 1.13)—though of course that level of interpretation is valid in its own place. Who this man is can ultimately be grasped only by going beyond the processes of nature and history altogether. His explanation or origin, says John, lies in the principle or 'word' of God behind it all. For he is the self-expression of that divine activity that all along has been coming into its own, first in nature, then in a people, and finally now fully embodied in a person. And, so perfect a reflection of it is he that the analogy that comes to John's mind is that which we use when we say of a boy that he is the spit-image of his father—or in the Hebrew metaphor, the 'glory (or reflection) as of a father's only son' (John 1.14. In the Greek at this point, unlike the English versions, there are no articles or capitals: it is a simile from human relationships). So John speaks of Jesus as the Word who 'is God what God is' (1.1), as 'God's only Son' or even (and here, as I said earlier, is where the latest papyrus discovery could finally have tilted the balance in favour of the most difficult reading) 'the only one (who is) himself God' (1.18). Yet his opening chapter also goes on to rehearse those more traditionally Jewish titles which the other Gospels give him: 'God's Chosen One' (1.34, the reading adopted in the NEB text); 'the Messiah' or Christ (1.41); 'the Son of God, the king of Israel' (1.49).

Now all these are titles which occur on the lips of others. In the prologues it is the Church speaking, filling out *its* answers to the question, Who is this man?, and preparing the reader to understand the story that follows. These were the categories, 'a Saviour, who is Christ, the Lord' (Luke 2.11), in which the Church preached Jesus from the earliest days (Acts 2.36), and subsequently they expanded their understanding of him in such terms as the pre-existent 'image' or 'son' of God (see, for instance, Rom. 1.3f; 2 Cor. 4.4f; Phil. 2.5–11; Col.

1.15–20). But what relation does all this exalted language bear to anything that Jesus may have thought or claimed for himself?

This is a relevant question for a Church that deliberately undertook to write Gospels—a form of literature with no exact precedent or parallel elsewhere. Had the first Christians simply confined themselves (as did the Qumran community) to documents setting out their message or reinforcing their teaching, then the question of what relation if any that bore to what Jesus said or did would be secondary and perhaps irrelevant. But for the gospel they preached about him they appealed with open eyes to the gospel *he* preached when he came into Galilee proclaiming, 'The time has come; the kingdom of God is upon you' (Mark 1.15). And they proceeded to tell the story of what he taught and did and suffered and of how he was vindicated out of death. The second part of that story we shall look at in the next chapter, but what of the first?

Does it matter what Jesus thought of himself or what he said and did? Does it matter whether the Church got him right or wrong? Evidently the early Christians thought so, but have we any means of knowing or testing, or are we simply confined to their witness?

THE MESSAGE OF JESUS
The obvious thing would have been for them to have made Jesus merely the mouthpiece of their preaching—to put back on to his lips, and claim his sanction for, everything that they said about him. But this, unexpectedly, is what we do not find. Let me illustrate.

As we have just seen, their summary of Jesus's proclamation was in terms of the imminent coming of 'the kingdom of God'. Now this is a phrase that is remarkably rare in pre-Christian Judaism, though of course it has its background in the whole Old Testament teaching of God as King. It does not for instance feature in the Dea Sea scrolls. Yet it was constantly on the lips of Jesus. So many of his teaching parables start: 'The kingdom of God is like this'. It was the explanation too which he gave of his actions: 'If it is by the finger of God that I drive out devils, then be sure that the kingdom of God has already come upon you' (Luke 11.20). 'Thy kingdom come' was the heart also of the prayer he gave his disciples (Matt. 6.10), and to the very last day of his life he was talking to them about it and looking forward to its breaking: 'I tell you this: never again shall I drink from the fruit of the vine until that day when I drink it new in the kingdom of God' (Mark 14.25). One would naturally therefore expect it to feature prominently in the Church's message. Yet it does not once appear in the early speeches of Acts, which, though clearly written up by Luke, show many signs in their primitive phraseology of being preaching summaries that go back far behind him. Nor, remarkably, does it occur more than a handful of times in the writings of Paul or John. Evidently it formed a very subordinate part of the first Christians' preaching and teaching. They spoke not so much of the Kingdom as of the Church (a word that by contrast only occurs twice on Jesus's lips and each time in the Gospel of Matthew alone with his strong interest in the Christian community and its problems); and rather than the breakthrough of the reign of God they preached 'Jesus and the resurrection' (Acts 17.18). This does not in the least mean that there was no connection or continuity between the two. Indeed their message was that what Jesus said God would do, this indeed he had done. The one announcement was proclaimed as fulfilled in the other, the further side of that mighty act of God which had inaugurated the new age and set the last things in motion. What is significant, however, is that they came to use a subtly different vocabulary for it. They did not for the most part take up Jesus's words or in recording them put their phrases back on to his lips. There seems to have been a reverence for the remembered speech and acts of Jesus which provided an inbuilt resistance to the temptation to make him merely their mouthpiece or puppet.

The same resistance is observable when we turn not to what he said about God but what he said about himself. Here the temptation would have been still stronger to make him claim precisely what they claimed of him. But again there is a remarkable difference. As we have seen, *they* proclaimed him as 'Lord' and 'Christ'—so much so that within a few years (and the process is virtually complete in the writings of Paul) 'Christ' becomes no longer a title, 'the Messiah' (as it still is in the Gospel of John—another mark of its primitiveness), but a proper name. But in the Gospels, though the titles 'Lord' and 'Christ' are used of Jesus by others, they are rare, and virtually never occur on his own lips. (Where they do, scholars are almost unanimous in thinking that they are not Jesus's own words—e.g., in Mark 9.41, 'If anyone gives you a cup of water to drink because you are *Christ's*,' a term which is not in any of the other parallel forms of this saying.) On the contrary, Jesus is evidently uncomfortable with the designation 'Messiah', because it could so quickly slide into the political claim to be 'king'. In Mark's version, so far from acclaiming Peter for saying 'You are the Christ' (as in Matt. 16.17–19, verses which scholars have convincingly argued to be authentic but misplaced), Jesus rebukes him and shuts him up, turning at once to speak of 'the Son of Man' who must suffer and die (Mark 8.30–3).

Now this last title is the most mysterious of all. It occurs once on the lips of the dying Stephen in Acts 7.56, but *never* in the Church's preaching or teaching, either in Acts or the Epistles (though it *could* lie behind Paul's teaching about Christ as the new or heavenly Man). Yet in the Gospels it occurs scores of times—but always and only on the lips of Jesus (and again this applies equally to the Fourth Gospel, except when in 12.34 the crowds ask, as well they might, Who is this 'Son of Man' you are always talking about?). Even at the end of the first chapter of St John, when all the other titles have been used *of* him, this is the first and only one used *by* him (1.51). There is no clearer indication that while the early Christians may have made little or nothing of it, they still remembered and preserved Jesus's own distinctive vocabulary. What he himself *meant* by 'the Son of Man' is one of the most disputed issues of New Testament interpretation. I suspect it was used by him partly because it was a parable in itself: it did not carry an easily understood or misunderstood meaning. But it challenged faith and loyalty to one who (like the figure of a son of man in Dan. 7.13–22, a human being representing 'the saints of the Most High' or true people of God) could come to vindication and receive the kingdom only through and out of humiliation and suffering.

The early Christians, of course, saw Jesus as the Son of Man who *was* now vindicated to the throne of God as he said he would be. There is reason to think that they subsequently reapplied his words about 'coming on the clouds' (which at his trial in Mark 14.62 fit admirably with their original reference in Daniel to a coming *to* God in victory out of oppression) to their own expectation (placed on his lips in Mark 13.26) of a coming *from* God to round off everything. This is all part of the complex question of how far titles of glory (like predictions of resurrection) can be used as reliable evidence of how Jesus himself thought and spoke *before* the event. The safest assumption is to suspect that these may indeed be heightened and read back in the telling—despite the reverence of which we spoke for the remembered words of Jesus. Or let us say that 'remembering' was not for the early Christians just a neutral exercise in recalling facts. It was, as Jesus's words 'Do this in remembrance of me' indicate, or the promise, according to John, that the Holy Spirit would bring everything to the disciples' 'remembrance', a recalling of the past in such a way that did not leave it in the dead past but recreated it as present experience at a deeper level. The sayings and actions of the historical Jesus 'spoke' to them as words and deeds of the living Christ in and through the Church. Yet, as John also insists, the Holy Spirit would not speak 'of himself', inventing and creating out of nothing: he would take the things of Jesus and show them in a new and living light.

This is the process that above all we see at work in the Fourth Gospel itself. It is seeing and showing everything 'from the end'—not inventing or creating, but holding everything up for the true light to shine through it, so that *in* the flesh we can see the 'glory'. John's Gospel is not unhistorical but *history really entered into*. As Browning made him say in *A Death in a Desert*, which William Temple called 'the most penetrating interpretation of St John that exists in the English language', 'What first were guessed as points, I now knew stars'. And this process is not unique to the Fourth Gospel: it is occurring in all the Gospels, though usually not so consciously or profoundly. We may trace it in regard to the question, Who is this man?, by showing in greater detail how the titles of glory used by the Church to account for Christ's person, though in their present form the product of its reflection, are the 'stars' that show the 'points'. They draw out and light up what was implicit in the work and words of Jesus and what in his life-time was expressed more in terms of verbs than of nouns, in things he did rather than in claims that he made for himself.

THE PERSON OF CHRIST

It could indeed be said that Jesus claimed nothing for himself but everything for what God was doing through him. The one thing that is certain is that he did not go around 'saying he was God' (as in the old knock-down argument: 'If he said he was God, then *either* he was God *or* he was a bad man'—and the latter can be ruled out). Yet all our sources agree saints of the Most High' or true people of God) 14.63f and parallels; John 19.7), for 'making himself God' (John 10.33–6)—not, however, as far as our evidence goes, for arrogating to *himself* the name of God but precisely for speaking without so much as a 'Thus saith the Lord'. This is epitomised in his characteristic and distinctive form of address, 'Amen, I say to you', which, it has been well remarked, contains the whole of Christology in a nutshell. While a pious Jew concluded his prayer with an 'Amen', thus expressing his faith that God would act, Jesus prefaces his words with an 'Amen', thus identifying God with what he would say. In overruling and re-editing the Law with his astonishing contrast 'You have heard that it was said *to* the men of old (i.e., by God—not *by* them, as in the AV) ..., but I say to you' (Matt. 5.33, etc.), in forgiving sins, in quelling the spirits of evil and powers of nature, he steps in the eyes of his contemporaries into the space reserved for God. He refuses to 'make room' for God. He says that men's attitude to him will decide God's attitude to them. He invites men to come to him for life and rest—but always to himself as God's representative. It is impossible to escape the conclusion that he went around not just talking *about* God (that would not have provoked the reaction he did) but standing in God's place, acting and speaking for him. 'Take away every hint of this,' it has been said, 'and you are left with a blank.'

Yet this is no vocation to usurp or replace God. Jesus's utter dependence on the Father remains unquestioned, and nowhere more than in the Fourth Gospel. It is the vocation to represent him, the fearful calling to play God, to live God, to *be* him to men. And it is the more fearful because this does not mean what we mean by 'playing God', lording it over others, manipulating their lives. Precisely the opposite: it means identifying with them in suffering, serving love. It is putting oneself completely at their disposal—like the son in the parable of the wicked husbandmen in whom the patrimony is vested, and who therefore more than any other invites elimination; for he alone stands between men and God. As St John interprets it, there is no need to look beyond Jesus: he who has seen him has seen the Father.

Yet the one who is seen is utterly and completely *a man*. (This indeed was the offence: 'You a mere man, make yourself God'—John 10.33.) The real point of difference was not that he was not human, but is expressed again in the analogy of the same parable of the wicked husbandmen. The servants and the son are equally human (one is not a heavenly being dressed up), but they stand in decisively different relationship to the owner. Nothing describes Jesus's claim better than this relationship of 'sonship' which he lived out in everything he did and was, beginning with his address of the unutterable God by the blasphemously familiar *abba* (at any rate one critically unshakeable word that he spoke!). And sonship in the New Testament is in the first instance a parable from human relationships. Jesus used the difference between a servant and a son in several of his stories—not only in that just quoted but in that of the prodigal son ('I am no longer fit to be called your son; treat me as one of your paid servants') and in what must be recognised as the parable of the servant and the son in John 8.35: 'A servant has no permanent standing in the household, but a son belongs to it always'. I describe it in this way because in the English versions it is translated as '*the* son', and in the next verse the parable is indeed specifically applied to Jesus: 'If then the Son sets you free, you will be free indeed'. But originally this language speaks of ordinary human situations, as Dodd has also shown to be the case in what he calls the parable of the apprentice in John 5.19f: 'A son can do nothing on his own; he only does what he sees his father doing. What father does, son does; for a father loves his son and shows him all his trade'. For the evangelist indeed this is an allegory about 'the Father' and 'the Son', but for Jesus it was almost certainly a parable like the rest. Jeremias has convincingly argued that this is true also of what has been called 'the Synoptic thunderbolt from the Johannine sky' in the 'Q' tradition in Matt. 11.27 and Luke 10.22. It has rightly seemed improbable to critics that Jesus could really have used the language of later

Church theology like 'No one knows the Son except the Father and no one knows the Father except the Son'. But the 'the' is here to be seen as the same 'the' that we regularly find in parables, as in 'the sower went forth to sow' or 'who is the faithful and wise steward?' English idiom would use the indefinite article: 'As only a father knows his son, so only a son knows his father.' It is this analogy of the intimate and unique relationship between father and son which Jesus is claiming for himself. The capitalising of it into talk of 'the Father' and 'the Son' is part of the process of seeing 'stars' for 'points'. Yet the fact that it has already happened in the tradition lying behind both Matthew and Luke shows how far it goes back. A high Christology, as we know from Paul, was very primitive.

If this is the kind of process at work in all the Gospels, synoptic and Johannine, it warns us that we must be prepared to discount as the work of Christian reflection the theologising to be found in the language and the titles used of Jesus (reserved as this use still is in comparison with the Epistles). But it also enables us to see that this talk was not just the invention or creation of the Church. What it did was to take up the enormous *implicit* claims of Jesus's language, and still more of his actions, and to make them explicit. Who this man was was a man (and there was no question or doubt about *that*—least of all in John who uses the word 'man' of Jesus twice as often as all the other Gospels put together) who yet stood in a unique relationship to God, speaking and acting for him. He was 'the man who lived God', his representative, his plenipotentiary to whom 'everything was entrusted' (Matt. 11.27)—and yet who was and could do nothing 'in himself' (John 5.30).

This paradox comes out most forcibly in what the New Testament calls his 'mighty works'. These too are essentially bound up for the Gospel writers with the question, Who is this man? (Mark 4.41). And they are inseparable from his teaching: 'What is this? A new kind of teaching! He speaks with authority. When he gives orders, even the unclean spirits submit' (Mark 1.27). For us the question of what we call the 'miracles' takes the form of asking 'Did they really happen, and if so how?'. A miracle is thought of as something that breaks or suspends a law of nature. But the men of the first century had no idea of laws of nature; for them the issue did not turn at all on the question of How? Even if in our sophistication we may have more understanding of how, psychosomatically, some of the healing miracles may have been effected, it would not make any difference to their being in the New Testament sense 'miracles', that is (from the Latin *mirari*), wonderful works or supremely gracious acts of God. For to Jesus's contemporaries the issue turned on the question not How? but Who? 'By whose power, in whose name, are you doing this?', 'By whom do your sons cast them out?' Whether therefore such acts (whether of Jesus or others) would now be called miracles, or whether they were inevitably described and written up as such, or exaggerated by a credulous age, is entirely secondary—though these are legitimate questions for *us* to ask and to which to apply our critical tools. We may take a different view of many of them, and we shall, or should, want to discriminate here as elsewhere, not dogmatically believing the lot or dismissing the lot, but sifting the processes at work in the telling and transmission of them.

It is worth interjecting that there is a false discrimination as well as a true. It is natural to the conservatism of the committed in all of us to retain as much as we can with the minimum of mental effort and to bring in critical considerations to explain or smooth away only what we find difficult (particularly the so-called 'nature' miracles in contrast with the healing miracles). But this is to give the impression of 'special pleading'—which in fact it is. Consider, for instance, the highly problematic cursing of the barren fig tree (Matt. 21.18–22; Mark 11.12–14, 20–4). Taken literally, it seems to present a petulant Jesus losing his temper with a tree for not having fruit out of season. It is obvious from the context that this was not the point of the story for those who told it. It is evidently an acted parable, in the tradition of the Old Testament prophets, of judgement against Israel (for which the fig tree like the vineyard was a stock symbol) which only had leaves to show and no fruit. It is set in the context of a prophetic action (the cleasing of the temple) and a parable (of the wicked husbandmen) that make the same point. Indeed in the independent Lukan tradition there is also a *parable* of a fig tree with a similar message (Luke 13.6–9). Whether Jesus actually did anything, and if so what, we shall never know for certain. It could be that a spoken warning or an act of prophetic symbolism has been turned into a miracle. In any case the story has to do with the moral character not of Jesus but of Israel. The point, however, is that we cannot bring these considerations in only when things become difficult, and then expect to be credible. All the stories have to be judged by the same theological and literary criteria. We must ask these questions not only to get out of our difficulties but to get into their meaning. For, as John says (and again he is but drawing out what is implicit in the others), they are 'signs'.

Yet signs of what? The older type of Christian apologetic used to use the miracles as proofs that Jesus was God, or at least the Christ. But this is to misrepresent the New Testament. In his day there were wonder-workers enough (as there are faith-healers today), and casting out demons was no exclusive prerogative of the Messiah—even the followers of Jesus's opponents did that (Luke 11.19; Matt. 12.27). The issue was, Whose power were you using? And Jesus is never represented as using or claiming his own power. But 'if it is', he says, 'by the finger of *God* that I drive out the devils, then be sure the kingdom of God has already come upon you' (Luke 11.20; Matt. 12.28). John's Gospel brings out precisely the same point. The 'works' are done entirely in the Father's power. Indeed, if Jesus said or did anything in his own name, there was no reason why the Jews should take any notice of him: they would be right to reject him. Always Jesus makes it clear that it is to God, not to him, that 'all things are possible' (Mark 10.27), and that this power is available to everyone who has faith (Mark 9.23). The response to the healing of the paralytic is typical: 'The people ... praised God for granting such authority to men' (Matt. 9.8). The furthest even Matthew with his heightening of the supernatural makes Jesus go is to say in Gethsemane: 'Do you suppose that I cannot appeal to my Father, *who* would at once send to my aid more than twelve legions of angels?' (Matt. 26.53). There is no suggestion that he himself could lay them on *because he was God*. He is a man of power because he is a man of prayer. But because he is a man of prayer, he knows also it is not the Father's will to win that way.

This picture of one who in utter faith and obedience is the Father's agent, and *therefore* the supreme representative of his love and power, is one that comes through all the Gospels. John merely draws it out in the paradox that he is completely one with the Father *because* the Father is greater than he (John 10.29f; 14.28). And he does this by stressing more than the others *both* Jesus's total dependence (as the one 'sent') *and* his complete freedom and intimacy with the Father. There is nothing he has that is not the Father's—and therefore nothing the Father has that is not his. The *way* in which he draws this out—when Jesus speaks, for instance, of the glory that he had with the Father before the world began (John 17.5)—often makes it sound as if Jesus for him was not a genuine historical human being at all. But that would be completely to misinterpret and misrepresent him. It would deny all that he has to say about the Word being made *flesh*. Such language is not to be taken at the level of psychological verisimilitude, of what he is most likely actually to have said (that would make Jesus a madman, as indeed the Jews, who do take it at this level, frequently say), but of theological verity, of what deep down is the truth lying behind him and his person. For the truth about this man is not to be exhausted by his physical origins. At that level, of course, he comes 'from Nazareth', and as a historical individual he is no more pre-existent than you or I. (Lack of discrimination at this point has done a good deal in Christian theology to throw doubt on his humanity.) But as the embodiment of the self-expressive activity of God, as 'the Word', he goes back before John the Baptist (John 1.15), before Isaiah (12.41), before Abraham (8.58), and indeed before creation itself (1.1f; 17.5, 24). John never confuses the two levels (people like

111

Nicodemus do that), but like a television or film producer he 'mixes' or superimposes his pictures, with great dramatic effect and often with irony and *double entendres*.

If we do not distinguish the levels at which the New Testament writers are speaking and take the language of pre-existence like the language of myth and legend *literally*, as the sort of thing you might have heard if you had been around with a tape-recorder, then we have only ourselves to blame—though we do not only have ourselves to put off. But if we can learn to trust the New Testament for what it is trying to say, rather than for what it is not trying to say, then we may find ourselves concurring with the claim of St John as much as any of the others, that 'his witness is true'—the real, inner truth *of* the history.

7

WHAT CAME OF HIM?

IF the question from which the Gospels begin, and
indeed which they continue to pose throughout, is
Who is this man?, the question to which they lead
up and which dominates their second half is What
came of him? In a real sense too this question is
there from the beginning, since they are all written
from the end, presupposing in everything they say
about him what came out. And the question What
came of him?, like the question Who is this man?,
has to be answered both at the historical and at the
theological level. In one sense it is a plain story with
the events of Jesus's life working themselves out to
their inevitable end, and to their utterly unex-
pected reversal on the third day, told with an attention to detail, a restraint and lack of doctrinal
elaboration which is remarkable. On the other
hand, 'what came of him' was theological through
and through: the Spirit, the Church, the new age,
the resurrection order—that total reality which led
Paul to exclaim: 'When anyone is united to Christ,
there is a new world; the old order has gone, and a
new order has already begun' (2 Cor. 5.17). And
that could only be described in language, like the
language of the birth narratives, which bursts the
bounds of factual description. Indeed there is no
description of the resurrection—that is left to the
apocryphal gospels. Naturally too the meaning
colours the facts themselves, and sometimes it is

difficult to know what is intended as interpretation and what as event. For instance, the rending of the temple-veil from top to bottom (and notice the symbolism of the direction) at the moment of Jesus's death (Mark 15.38), seen as destroying the barrier between man and God and declaring all things holy, is clearly a highly theological statement—whatever its factual basis, if any (and it has left no trace, amid many portents of the end, in Jewish records). Yet the amount of legendary material in the passion narratives is much less than in the birth stories. They were obviously controlled by the memory of what happened.

THE TRIAL AND DEATH OF JESUS

The story of the death of Jesus and of what led up to it and flowed from it, which occupies such a disproportionate space in the Gospels (a third of Mark and nearly a half of John), reflects the decisive importance for the early Christian preaching of the death and resurrection of Christ. It is *this* that dominates the early sermons of Acts and the Epistles—his birth is not mentioned and his ministry hardly at all (the most it rates is three verses in Acts 10.37–9). The disproportion, then, should not surprise us and it is clearly not determined by biographical considerations. What surely must surprise us, though, is the manner in which the subject is treated. We should not be led to expect, for instance, that the author of Acts was at all interested in the *story* of the passion. He follows up that curt summary of the ministry with the baldest possible account of Jesus's end: 'He was put to death by hanging on a gibbet; but God raised him to life on the third day' (10.40). Yet how wrong we should be! In fact it is almost certain that Luke takes the trouble to weave together two independent stories of the passion, one which he shares with Mark and Matthew and one from a separate source; and this latter has interesting points of contact with John's, again apparently independent, tradition.

For as well as their theological interest in the meaning of the events it is surely evident that the early Christians had an interest in the historical story for its own sake. The passion narrative in all the Gospels is the Achilles' heel (and it is a pretty large one) of the theory of many of the form-critics that the Church had no concern for the historical framework of Jesus' life. According to this view, individual units of tradition (miracle-stories, parables, pronouncements and the rest) were simply handed down like collections of loose pearls and the Christian communities neither knew nor cared how they fitted together. The connecting thread, supplied later by the evangelists or redactors, was topical and theological: it affords no confidence for reconstructing the order of events. I believe this to be a perverse and one-sided reading of the evidence, even of the pre-passion narrative. I am convinced that their theological interest did not cancel but rather controlled their historical interest —and that their historical interest did not cancel but rather controlled their theological interest.

This again may be illustrated supremely by the Fourth Gospel which, as well as being theologically the most profound, is full of historical and geographical details for which no plausible doctrinal or symbolic reason can be found. They are there because that is how it happened—though how it happened, and when, and where, is *also*, for those with the eyes to see *through* the details, of profound significance. Indeed, in a test-study I once did of time and place in the Gospel narratives John came off the best, and Luke, surprisingly, the worst. In Acts, where he knew and covered the ground, his detail is very sharp. His narrative of Palestine, which evidently he did not know, apart from the environs of Jerusalem and Caesarea, is often extraordinarily vague. But it is a tribute to him as a historian that where he does not know he does not invent: he generalises. John, however, gives us a much more detailed topographical and chronological framework of the ministry. It is very different from that which we could deduce from the Synoptists alone—beginning with a pre-Galilean ministry of Jesus alongside John the Baptist in Judaea and extending in all for at least three years and probably four. (The others mention only one Passover.) The Synoptic account can be fitted into it but not vice versa. When we come to the passion narrative there is a major divergence—John dating the death of Jesus before the Passover meal was eaten (John 18.28), the Synoptists treating the last supper the previous evening as the Passover meal (Mark 14.12) and thereby making the trial and crucifixion take place during the festival. The resolution of this problem is far too complex to go into here, and scholars of course differ; but I think it would be fair to say that a majority of English scholars would believe John to be right. Whatever Jesus and his friends may have observed as *their* Passover celebration, it is almost incredible that the arrest, trial and crucifixion of Jesus could have taken place during the public festival in blatant defiance of all its detailed regulations. It seems far more likely that the Pharisees and chief priests should have pressed to get it out of the way before the festival started, as John says. In any case at this and many other points it is clear that the evidence of the Fourth Gospel has to be taken very seriously, if not preferred. It is in the historical and not simply the theological business.

The passion narratives as a whole raise more issues than we can possibly treat here, but at one point in particular it is perhaps worth trying to correct a balance. For much recent popular writing has taken the line that the trial of Jesus is written up in a way that is largely propaganda rather than history. Two distorting tendencies have been detected. The first is an anti-Jewish bias, of seeking to throw all the guilt for the crucifixion on the Jews, while white-washing the Romans. The second is a rewriting of the evidence to disguise the fact that Jesus and his followers were hand in glove with the Jewish nationalist cause and to dissociate them from the revolt that failed in 66–70 (showing them again to be good citizens of the Roman Empire).

It is to be observed first, as I mentioned earlier, that the Roman historian Sherwin-White, who has studied the story of the trial, like the narrative of Acts, from the point of view of its accuracy on points of Roman law and social practice, gives it high marks. If the whole thing is a rewriting of history (on the Stalinist model), then the Church employed some very good historians. It is in fact the alternative scenarios which have been offered, of Passover plots and Zealot links, that are in my judgement the really tendentious readings of the evidence. It is notable that the Jewish historian Josephus had a very poor view of the Zealots but a very respectful view of Jesus and never suggests any connection between the two movements.

However, rather than criticise these theories in detail, I would simply invite the reader to compare the assessment to be found in Dodd's last book, *The Founder of Christianity*. This is how he sums up the situation that faced the Jews before the trial:

Jesus must be removed by death; he must also be

discredited. The death sentence therefore must be legally and formally pronounced by the governor. The surest way to secure such a sentence would be to cite the Defendant on a charge of political disaffection. But such a charge would by no means discredit him in the eyes of the Jewish public; quite the contrary. It was for the Sanhedrin to show that he was guilty of an offence against religion.

The one charge that met both these requirements was that of claiming to be the Messiah. This could be interpreted from the religious point of view as the blasphemous one of making himself the Son of God and from the political point of view as the seditious one of pretending to the throne of Israel. And the Gospels all agree on the fatal way in which these three terms, Christ, Son of God and King could slide, or be made to slide, into one another.

The first requirement of any satisfactory account of the trial of Jesus is that it should be able to show how the political charge, though recognised to be disingenuous, could still have seemed plausible. The strength of the interpretation that reads Jesus as a political revolutionary is that his position must have been *open* to the construction put upon it in Luke 23.2: 'We found this man subverting our nation, opposing the payment of taxes to Caesar and claiming to be Messiah, a King'. The weakness of such an interpretation is that it does not do justice to the evidence that everyone in the drama (the Jewish leaders, Pilate and Jesus himself) *knew* that this construction was fundamentally a lie.

This is nowhere again made clearer than in the Gospel of John. No one is arguing that the Johannine account of the trial or of anything else is primarily to be assessed by the canons of tape-recorded accuracy (though if there had been a tape in the Praetorium would it have put the issue beyond doubt or suspicion any more than the tapes in the White House?). That is indeed to judge things 'as the eyes see' rather than with true discernment. Nevertheless, the truth *of* the history is nowhere, I believe, at this point brought out better than in John. Not only is the reader appraised unequivocally of Jesus's own position: 'My kingdom does not belong to this world. If it did, my followers would be fighting to save me from arrest by the Jews' (John 18.36)—and this still remains a decisive reply to any such construction. But the disingenuousness of the Jewish religious leaders over their charge against Jesus is subtly conveyed. They begin their dealings with Pilate by trying to get away without having to be specific at all: 'Pilate went out to them and asked 'What charge do you bring against this man?'' "If he were not a criminal," they replied, "we should not have brought him before you"' (18.29f). When that fails, as it obviously must in a court of law, they go on for the capital charge of high treason (18.33–19.6). When Pilate finds no case on that one, they fall back on the real offence (for them) of his blasphemous claim to be the Son of God (19.7). Finally, with that getting them nowhere, they return to the political tack and outmanoeuvre Pilate with the utterly cynical claim of being more loyal to Caesar than he (19.12–16). So far from John's account being the end-term of an increasingly anti-semitic bias (he is after all a Jew writing to persuade Jews), it exactly preserves the balance of the earliest Christian summary, when Peter is made to say to the Jerusalem crowd on the day of Pentecost: 'You used heathen men to crucify and kill him' (Acts 2.23).

Whatever the interpretation, which of course is

just as much part of history as 'the facts', few historians (except those who claim from time to time to revive the desperate theory that Jesus never lived) would question the basic historicity of the arrest, crucifixion and burial of Jesus. Yet what came of him in the end does not stop there: if it had there would have been no story to tell and no Church to tell it. But when we move in the last chapter of the Gospels to the story of the resurrection we find ourselves apparently in a very different world. Is this the point at which history leaves us and theology, myth and legend alone take over? Certainly not, according to the claim of the whole New Testament. But how, and in what sense, are we to trust it at this point above all?

THE RESURRECTION

Let us be clear that belief in the resurrection is in the first place a judgement of faith. It expresses the conviction 'Jesus lives!', that he belongs not simply to the dead historical past but is a present spiritual reality. Now this is not a judgement that the historian *qua* historian can make or take away. To that extent the resurrection is on quite a different level from the crucifixion. No one in the New Testament claims to have seen it happen. The crucifixion of Jesus was a public event, witnessed by all and sundry, whatever they made of it. The evidence for the resurrection rests on those who believed in it, and, with the exception of the appearance to Paul, was given only to those who had previously known and accepted Jesus. Yet the claim of the entire New Testament is that on the third day *something happened*. And, as Paul says, this is the hinge-event on which the whole Christian witness turns: 'If Christ was not raised, then is our gospel null and void, and so is your faith' (1 Cor. 15.14). If nothing happened, there is no more to be said. The historical evidence is not decisive in the sense that it is all that is required. Yet it is decisive in the sense that if it could be exploded there would be a hole at the heart of the Christian faith. To use the philosophers' distinction, the historical evidence is not sufficient, but it is necessary. So what are we to make of it?

The evidence falls into three classes.

1. There is first, in order of what was seen, the evidence of the tomb found empty. This looks like the most solid piece of evidence of all. Here is something the historian can really get his hands on: either is was empty or it was not. And indeed, despite all its offence to our historical and scientific presuppositions, this is something that it is very hard to dismiss—so much so that for most people, as I discover from virtually every question I am asked on the subject, 'Do you believe in the resurrection?' *means* 'Do you believe in the empty tomb?'. Yet it comes as a surprise to most to be told that though the resurrection was the lynch-pin of Paul's whole gospel, never once does he mention the empty tomb nor does he appear to attach any significance to it. This is not to say that he knew nothing of it, let alone that he denied it. It is a false conclusion to draw from his silence that it was a story that was only invented later. On the contrary, his statement in 1 Cor. 15.3f of the gospel as he himself first received it, that 'Christ died ...; that he was buried; that he was raised to life on the third day', clearly presupposes some connection of the resurrection with the *tomb* and not simply with the visions of the living Christ, which alone he goes on to narrate and which on his account might, like his own, have taken place anywhere. Yet the fact that he does not take up this connection or stress its evidential value suggests

121

that it did not in itself have the significance that has since been attached to it. In the Gospels too it is notable that the empty tomb as such convinces no one, except one man, who looking back in faith, 'saw and believed' (John 20.8). Everyone else saw and was dismayed: by itself it persuaded no one.

There is a school of New Testament scholars who argue that the empty tomb story is a subsequent creation of the Church's faith because this is what in Jewish hope 'resurrection' must have implied: believing on other grounds, the early Christians necessarily depicted it thus. But in fact it would have meant nothing of the sort. It would have meant a rising of the dead at the last day for final judgement—which is what the term 'the resurrection', in contrast with temporary resuscitation, always continues to mean in the Gospels (e.g., in Mark 12.23, 'at the resurrection, when they come back to life, whose wife will she be?'). And the classic Old Testament image for this coming back to life was the breathing of life *into* dead bones (Ezek. 37.1–14). That there would be a grave empty in the middle of history with no bones in it at all was not what *anyone* expected. Moreover, if the story of the empty tomb had really been invented to convince doubters, the Church would surely have made a better job of it. Except in the Fourth Gospel, it rested entirely on the testimony of women (which in Jewish law was not binding and whose visions do not even rate inclusion in the Pauline list), and it did not involve the Apostles. In Mark (as far at any rate as the original text goes) the women did not tell them. In Luke they told them, but they disbelieved the report. In Matthew the women told them on Jesus's own instructions to leave for Galilee, and this they did without taking any action about the tomb. You do not develop—or even include—

stories merely to throw away their point. On the contrary, I would again agree with Dodd's assessment in *The Founder of Christianity*:

It looks as if they [the evangelists] had on their hands a solid piece of tradition, which they were bound to respect because it came down to them from the first witnesses, though it did not add much cogency to the message they wished to convey, and they hardly knew what use to make of it.

The evidence would suggest that while the finding of the grave empty was not invented by the early Church it neither created belief nor was created by it. It was simply part of what was indelibly remembered to have been discovered that morning. *Why* it was empty admits of no certain explanation, natural or supernatural. There are indeed some which can surely be ruled out as so improbable as to be incredible. In that class I would put deliberate fraud by the disciples (the best explanation, according to Matt. 28.12–15, that could be suggested by the Jews); or the theory that the women went to the wrong tomb and no one bothered to check (especially in the light of the women's careful observation in Mark 15.47); or that Jesus never really died but revived in the cool of the sepulchre (an old chestnut, raked up by D. H. Lawrence and many others. For even if he didn't die then, what happened to him? That he could just have lain low and disappeared passes belief); or that his corpse as that of a convict was simply dissolved in a lime-pit (the *burial* of Jesus is one of the best attested facts about him, being recorded in 1 Corinthians, all four Gospels and Acts). But the first and most obvious thought, namely, of foul play ('They' have 'taken him away'; John 20.2), cannot so easily be dismissed. In a situation or rival nationalist groups, still only too familiar in Palestine, extremist fanatics could have remedied the Governor's unusual decision to release the body by removing the corpse under cover of night to one of the criminals' graves. We shall never know for certain, and even the evidence of the grave-clothes in John 20.6f is *compatible* with their being left strewn around and bundled together. The fact that the body was not produced will never prove that it could not have been produced, any more than the absence of Hitler's corpse to this day proves that he rose from the dead. And in truth nothing *depends* on what happened to the old body. It may indeed have been subject to some molecular transformation unimaginable to us, but we can never be sure. Its disappearance, which at first produced doubt and dismay, was subsequently seen as a *sign* of what God had done. But the resurrection is not the shell of the cocoon but the butterfly. The bones of Jesus *could* yet be lying around Palestine and the resurrection still be true. For belief in it does not depend on—let alone consist of—the fact that they do not. The empty grave cannot of itself be decisive either way.

So we move to the second set of evidence.

2. What produced the faith—or at any rate turned the disciples around in their own tracks (quite literally in the Emmaus story) was not the tomb but the appearances. It is indeed very difficult to dismiss these and still find a credible explanation for the utter *volte face* that produced the Christian Church. Mere wish-fulfillment as an explanation (against all the evidence that they were wishing anything of the kind) is itself the last refuge of those who do not wish to believe. Again, to say that the whole Christian movement rested on deception and

yet survived without anyone exposing it from within or without is surely to stretch credulity. That *something* happened that was not purely hallucinatory (the equivalent of seeing pink rats) seems certain; and it is supported by the earliest possible witness—Paul's personal attestation of what was handed on to him within a few years of the crucifixion, which, as he says, could have been confirmed or confounded by many still living.

Yet Paul's detailed list differs considerably from those in the Gospel accounts, which in themselves diverge in regard both to the location of the appearances (Jerusalem or Galilee or both—Paul mentions no places) and to the degree of 'materialisation'. Above all, Paul appears to regard the rest of the appearances as belonging to the same class as his own on the Damascus road—a vision of the glorified Christ very different from that of a seemingly reconstituted quasi-physical body that could eat fish or pass through doors. That for Paul the resurrection body of Christians did *not* mean this is about as clear as it can be from his subsequent discussion in 1 Cor. 15—and what happened to Christ is seen as the first instalment or typical sample of what will happen to us. The one thing he can say for certain is that our resurrection body will not depend in any way on this body of flesh and bones—for 'on the day' it will make no difference at all whether, like the living, we have one or, like the dead, we do not. Any kind of physical continuity or reconstitution is (not of course impossible but) irrelevant.

Yes if the 'appearances' belong, as in some sense they must, to the realm of paranormal psychology, or extra-sensory perception, then that there should be wide differences in the experiencing and in the reporting of them is scarcely an objection. In fact the divergences in the stories both of the tomb and of the visions are precisely the kind that one would expect in any authentic as opposed to concocted accounts. If the visions were veridical psychic phenomena, that is, genuine communications with the spirit-world, then the degree of materialisation and their location are neither here nor there: these will depend on the experiencing subject. The association of such phenomena especially with the period immediately following death, and with those who knew the dead man best, is certainly not incredible, however (still in these enlightened days) inexplicable. What is significantly different however is what they were taken to *mean*. This was not the temporary survival of a loved one (whether in the mind of the beholder or in some kind of etheric body) but resurrection; and by resurrection, not resuscitation (as in the case of Jairus's daughter or Lazarus) only to die again, but the abiding presence of a life-giving power, signalling a new world-order and the beginning of the End. And for *that* conviction the appearances may have been necessary triggers, but they were not and are not sufficient explanation.

3. It was this third strand in the evidence that was really decisive for the early Church. For belief in the resurrection was not confined to those who had seen the appearances, let alone to those who had viewed the tomb. It was founded not on other people's tall stories but on a corporate spiritual awareness of Christ no longer as a dead memory, however vivid, but as a vivifying presence. When Paul spoke to his converts, who like himself had never met Jesus, of knowing him and the fellowship of his sufferings and the power of his resurrection (Phil. 3.10), it was this fact of 'the new being' 'in Christ' to which he made his appeal. The appearances he appealed to for the credentials of his

own apostleship (1 Cor. 15.8–11), the empty tomb never.

The evidence for the resurrection is indeed strongest where it looks weakest and weakest where it looks strongest. The empty tomb, even if it could be certified empty and the shroud produced (and I regard the famous Shroud of Turin as by no means to be dismissed out of hand), would finally prove nothing: the body could still have been removed from it. The appearances have about them a large element of subjectivity and at best add up to a reasonably well-attested case of temporary survival: they certainly do not of themselves spell resurrection. The ongoing spiritual experience—this looks the most intangible fact of all. Yet without it the other two would not have been interpreted as they were and the Christian Church would not have been born, let alone survived. And this is the most incontrovertible historical fact of all. The historian in trying to compass the phenomenon is left at most with the linen garments in his hands, the tracks of a phantom across his pages, the external institution of the Christian Church. The inner reality escapes him, and it must, because, if it is true at all, it is a reality that belongs not to the level of flesh but of spirit. That Jesus *lives*, now, is a conviction that cannot finally be substantiated by any evidence from the past—only from the present.

Yet the resurrection is also claimed by the New Testament writers to be an event of history—as real as the crucifixion—and if the history is discredited the faith cannot but be eroded. There are indeed those who would be content to say that something happened, but only to the disciples: the rest is the language of symbolism and picture-story to describe the spiritual transformation that for them turned the cross from defeat into victory. Now clearly there is such a function in the language they used, as in the language they used in telling the stories of the birth of Jesus or his ascension. In fact most thinking Christians would now agree that (whatever its historical basis) the ascension *story* is primarily to be seen as a symbolic representation of the spiritual truth that Christ is not only alive but Lord: it describes his ascendency from now on, not a moment in time or a movement in space. But here the language employed—of angels and clouds and going up in glory—is stock symbolism (derived largely from the Old Testament) whose significance everyone at the time would have understood. There is indeed some of this also in the resurrection stories, particularly in the introduction, and multiplication, of angelic figures, whose recognised literary function, as at the birth of Jesus, is to interpret events of otherwise such doubtful interpretation as acts of God. But I am not persuaded that it is so easy to explain away the other language, of spices and stones and sweat-bands. This was never part of a stock of symbolic imagery and would not have been taken for such.

If the resurrection story has a foot in *public* history (and to abandon that claim is to abandon something that has been central to the entire Christian tradition), then it must be open and vulnerable to the historian's scrutiny. Never let us suppose that we need not bother with his questions or that we are impervious to them. This is part of the risk of a religion of the Word made flesh—in Winston Churchill's phrase its 'soft under-belly'. And though the historian can neither give nor directly take away the faith, he can indirectly render the credibility-gap so wide that in fact men cease believing. My trust in the New Testament accepts that risk. That is why as a New Testament scholar I am convinced that it is important to be a good historian as well as a man of faith—and not to confuse the two by giving answers of faith where historical evidence alone is relevant. For *if* Jesus could really be shown to be the sort of man who went into hiding rather than face death, or just another nationalist or freedom-fighter with a crime-sheet of violence, or the leader of a movement which rested in the last analysis on fraud, then I can think of other candidates in reply to Peter's question, 'Lord, to whom else shall we go?' (John 6.68). The answers that history can give will never take us all the way—and at best they cannot be more than highly probable. Exactly what happened at the tomb, or anywhere else, we shall never know. All we can ask—and must require—for faith, for the response of Thomas, 'My Lord and my God!', is that the credibility-gap be not too wide. And that assurance I am persuaded—or I would not remain a Christian—is what the history, after all the sifting of the best and most rigorous scholarship, can sustain.

8

TRUSTFUL FAITH

CAN we trust the New Testament? I firmly believe
we can. But trust it for what? For a faith-ful record,
in both senses of that phrase. And what, as I see it,
that involves may be summarised by comparison
again with the responses of the four attitudes from
which we began.

'The cynicism of the foolish' believes that because the New Testament record is full of faith in
one sense it cannot be faithful in the other. It is indeed full of faith, throbbing with the Church's conviction about Jesus as the Christ, the Son of God,
Lord of the living and dead. But an integral part of
the Christ of faith is the Jesus of history. For it is
faith in the Word made *flesh*. We have seen reason
to believe that the first Christians had a reverence
for the remembered words and deeds of Jesus which
refused to allow them to make of him simply the
mouthpiece of their own message. If they had been
shown to have falsified, they would have been the
first to admit with St Paul that they were 'lying witnesses' or with St John that 'the truth is not in us'.
And where we are able to check them against non-
Christian sources or the contemporary background
of Roman or Jewish society there is good reason to
conclude that the Gospels and Acts are not fictional
records, far removed from fidelity to fact. To despair of knowing anything or of having any objective
criteria is faithlessness to the very scientific and his-

torical method to which such critics would trust in every other field. I believe we must meet and challenge them on their own ground.

On the other hand, 'the fundamentalism of the fearful' will not admit the right of this method to the freedom in which alone it can function. It may 'use' it within a limited field for its own ends, and it does not hesitate to claim its 'results' when it suits them. But the ends are not open—and any results are thereby discredited. Its faith is not a trustful one. It is blinkered, and for this reason insecure. The revival of fundamentalism in our day, though psychologically understandable when all is shifting, is ultimately, I believe, a liability to the truth it claims to defend. For truth cannot be defended by such means. And the personal truth, above all, of which the gospel speaks is not to be comprehended or safeguarded by the infallibility of either a book or a pope. Yet the fear which feeds this attitude can only be cast out by love—and by the discovery that ultimately there is no need for it. This *is* happening —it has happened dramatically in the field of Roman Catholic scholarship—and in my experience the first step in the cure for such defensiveness is not to threaten it. But in the long run, as the many signs of first-class research coming from this camp are beginning to show, the only answer is better and more faithful scholarship. Then the laager of fear will be found unnecessary.

With 'the scepticism of the wise' we come to the first of two attitudes with which I at least have considerable sympathy. It *is* open and it is often combined with real faithfulness and genuine devotion to Christ. My criticism would be that it is needlessly distrustful. In his *New Testament Theology* Jeremias formulates the following 'principle of method': 'In the synoptic tradition it is the inauthenticity and not the authenticity of the sayings of Jesus that must be demonstrated.' With every proper regard for the differences of aim, I would ask why this principle needs to be qualified with the words 'in the synoptic tradition'. As authenticity is understood in John (which is certainly not literalistically), I believe that it is just as applicable to his material. From a sustained study of the evidence I am not persuaded that one must assume that the early Church is not to be trusted on the sayings, or the deeds, of Jesus until proved otherwise. We have means of checking and discriminating and by those tests we can discern and discount the influences at work. To a good extent we can see where 'points' become 'stars', and why and how. Scepticism, or suspension of belief, has its place, and constant reminder that in the last analysis on any historical question one is dealing only with degrees of probability is a healthy contribution. Yet the scepticism of the wise—I will not call it 'the treason of the clerks'—has undoubtedly had its part in creating the unhealthy gap between the professor and the parson, the study and the pew. More understanding —and more love—on both sides is needed. And that again is achieved by sympathetic and accepting openness—not by dismissive reviews and sniping articles.

Finally, 'the conservatism of the committed' is an attitude that certainly I do not wish to knock. It exhibits that self-rectifying balance and solidity which has enabled English scholarship, as well as English religion, to weather the extremes of Continental radicalism and Transatlantic fashion. I believe too that more often than not it has been proved right— even if for wrong or muddled reasons. Yet it is not on the whole a trustful faith. It is suspicious of the wise and heavily biased towards those who come up with 'reassuring' answers—such as mine on the early dating of the New Testament or the apostolic authorship of the Fourth Gospel! In Kierkegaard's analogy, its attitude to truth is like swimming with one foot on the bottom—rather than trusting yourself over 70,000 fathoms. For those who cannot swim it is certainly better than that of fundamentalism—which keeps both feet flatly on the bottom. But a *Church* that cannot swim is in spiritual peril. For it is not free to obey its Lord's command to launch out into the deep. And if too many of its members, let alone its instructors, are in that condition, it will not be able to survive, let alone give a lead, in the modern world. This applies of course to much more than the New Testament. But if it cannot exhibit a trustful and critical faith in relation to *that*—the charter of its salvation—it will be fatally weakened at source.

The conclusion of the matter may be put quite simply. A Christian has nothing to fear but the truth. For it alone could show that this movement is not of God (Acts 5.38f). But he also has nothing to fear in the truth. For to him the truth *is* Christ (John 14.6). It is large—larger than the world—and shall prevail. It is also a living, and a growing, reality. And therefore he is free, or should be free, to follow the truth *wherever* it leads. He has no advance information or inbuilt assurance precisely where it will lead. I know that I have been led through the study of the New Testament to conclusions, both negative and positive, that I did not expect. For instance, just what underlies the birth narratives, what were the relations between the movements of John the Baptist and Jesus, how and in what way did Jesus's own understanding of his role become modified by events, how did he think of the future, did he expect to return, what is most likely to have happened at his trial and resurrection, what is the relative priority for the portrait of Jesus of our different sources, especially of the Fourth Gospel, what pattern and time-scale of early church development emerges from the dating of our documents?—on these and many other things my own mind has changed and will doubtless continue to change. And my picture will not be quite the same as anyone else's—more radical at some points, more conservative at others. There is nothing fixed or final: our knowledge and our questions are constantly expanding and shifting. And who knows what new evidence may not suddenly be dug up? Yet out of all this my trust in the primary documents of the Christian faith has been strengthened rather than shaken. The scholarship does not give me the faith; but it increases my confidence that my faith is not misplaced. Yet it provides no copper-bottomed guarantee. For the Christian walks always in this life by trust, and not by sight. And he is content to close his *Te Deum*, his most confident affirmation of faith, with the prayer of vulnerability: 'O Lord, in thee have I *trusted*: let me never be confounded.'

FOR FURTHER READING

IF you can't read the big books, read books by the big men. I have therefore selected a few which are mostly popularisations by major New Testament scholars or introductions by men who are themselves creative workers in the field. Selection is inevitably invidious, and I have been forced to omit all commentaries on individual books. These and many others by a wide range of publishers are included in the most useful catalogue, *Religion and Theology: A Select Book Guide*, issued annually from the SCM Bookroom, 58 Bloomsbury Street, London WC1B 3QX, through which also the books here mentioned may be ordered.

A. E. Harvey, *Companion to the New Testament*
> Commissioned to interpret the *New English Bible* to the general reader. The *Companion to the Gospels* section is available separately.

S. C. Neill, *The Interpretation of the New Testament 1861–1961*
> A survey of the historical development of modern criticism, with a special interest in the personalities involved.

A. M. Hunter, *Introducing the New Testament*
> A simple guide to the content, date and authorship of the writings.

W. D. Davies, *Invitation to the New Testament*

A longer guide by a creative scholar, written for laymen and dedicated to his teen-age daughter.

C. F. D. Moule, *The Birth of the New Testament*

A scholarly but readable description of what were the forces and circumstances that created a 'New Testament'.

C. H. Dodd, *The Apostolic Preaching and its Developments*

A classic investigation of what the earliest Christianity was and how both Epistles and Gospels grew out of 'the gospel'.

C. H. Dodd, *The Founder of Christianity*

The distillation of a major scholar's work on the life and teaching of Jesus.

C. L. Mitton, *Jesus: the Fact behind the Faith*

A forceful reply to the 'scepticism of the wise' on what we can know of the historical Jesus.

A. M. Hunter, *Interpreting the Parables*

A popularisation of the findings of recent New Testament scholarship in this field.

R. H. Fuller, *Interpreting the Miracles*

A parallel book on the miracles, concentrating on their theological significance.

J. Jeremias, *The Prayers of Jesus*

A demonstration of how a front-rank scholar examines, for instance, the Lord's Prayer and Jesus's language about God as Father.

A. M. Hunter, *According to John*

A summary of the new look on the Fourth Gospel over recent years.

J. Knox, *The Humanity and Divinity of Christ*

Mature reflections of a great interpreter of the New Testament on how its writers sought to understand Jesus.

H. J. Richards, *The First Christmas: What Really Happened?*
The Miracles of Jesus: What Really Happened?
The First Easter: What Really Happened?

Popular presentations by a Roman Catholic teacher of the New Testament, stressing the positive peace of the symbolic.

INDEX